ONE GIRL'S JOURNEY OF HOME, LOSS, AND HOPE

MY FAMILY DIVIDED

DIANE GUERRERO

WITH ERICA MOROZ

SQUARE
FISH

HENRY HOLT AND COMPANY
NEW YORK

SQUARE
FISH

An imprint of Macmillan Publishing Group, LLC
120 Broadway, New York, NY 10271
mackids.com

Square Fish and the Square Fish logo are trademarks of Macmillan and
are used by Henry Holt and Company under license from Macmillan.

Our books may be purchased in bulk for promotional, educational, or business use. Please
contact your local bookseller or the Macmillan Corporate and Premium Sales Department
at (800) 221-7945 ext. 5442 or by email at MacmillanSpecialMarkets@macmillan.com.

All photographs courtesy of Diane Guerrero

Library of Congress Cataloging-in-Publication Data is available.
ISBN 978-1-250-30878-8 (paperback)   ISBN 978-1-250-13487-5 (ebook)

Originally published in the United States by Henry Holt and Company
First Square Fish edition, 2019
Book designed by Liz Dresner
Square Fish logo designed by Filomena Tuosto

10   9   8   7   6

AR: 5.4 / LEXILE: 730L

For all the lonely hearts, know that you beat,
and that's all that matters.

INTRODUCTION

eported. Long before I understood the meaning of that word, I'd learned to dread it. It implied that one day, my loving, hardworking immigrant parents could be expelled from America and sent back to Colombia. Month after month, year after year, they strived to become American citizens. They pleaded, planned, and prayed. Their dream was to stay with me, here in the country we love.

My story is far from unique—in fact, it's heartbreakingly common. There are more than eleven million undocumented immigrants in America, according to US Immigration and Customs Enforcement (ICE). Often, they are fleeing the violence, poverty, and starvation that plague their home countries. America is a promised land, they hope, that will provide them with safety and solace.

For immigrants without legal documentation, the risk of being deported looms. It threatens to tear them away from their communities, their families, and—as in my family—their children. Some of the children who are left behind are placed in state care or foster families; many others are left on their own, like I was. After my parents were snatched away, no cop or government official checked up on me. No one seemed to care—or even notice—that I was alone.

Documented, detained, deported. These are things I never really understood as a kid—things that were rarely talked about. So, I wanted to give you the simplest way I can explain what these words mean. Here goes . . . What exactly do these words mean, and how do they work? Well, in order to live in this country legally, individuals need documents—such as birth certificates, visas, or green cards—that prove they were either born here or have government approval to stay. Some immigrants receive temporary visas, allowing them to live in the country for a set number of months or years. Other immigrants are granted residency, allowing them to work and live here legally. And still others are granted citizenship, which gives them the additional privileges of voting, serving on juries, and running for political office.

ICE is the government wing that enforces these laws. Their job is to arrest and detain (or, imprison) the people who have been living in the country without such documentation. Once an undocumented person is detained, a judge determines whether they will be deported and sent back to their homeland. The fear of this happening to my family shook us all to our cores. Anything, from the whir of a police siren down the block to the simple ring of our doorbell, was enough to make us panic. Who was there, and were they coming to take us away?

While we're at it, let's address some other vocab: I cringe every time I hear the phrase *illegal immigrant* or *illegal alien*. Since the only difference between immigrants and citizens is paperwork, *undocumented* makes more sense. It's also more respectful; no one is "illegal" in this world—we are all humans!

I wish I had understood these things at the time. It would have helped a lot. Honestly, if you're reading this book, you're already miles ahead of most of the people in this country who do not understand the immigration system and don't want to learn about it, because it seemingly doesn't affect them. Believe me, it affects all of us. It affects how safe we feel, the food we eat, and our friends and neighbors. Growing up, I kept my story a secret, and many of my friends and classmates had no idea what I was going through until my first book was published.

Talking about what happened to my family is difficult after years trying to hide it. So why open up now, nearly twenty years later? Because growing up, I felt like the only kid who'd ever dealt with having the people I loved most in the world snatched away from me. It would've meant everything to know that someone, somewhere, had survived what I was going through. For the thousands of nameless kids and teenagers who feel forgotten like I did—this memoir is for you. It's as much for your healing as it is for my own. In my neighborhood growing up, the sense of community between Latin American immigrants was strong. I want that community to reach across the whole country—standing together for what is right.

The forty-fifth president's administration is not making life easy for immigrant people. No, in fact, the administration is going out of its way to make it as difficult as possible, with a plan to increase border security, build a wall, and threaten innocent individuals and families with deportation.

Luckily, many, many people disagree with that dude in the White House. Immigrants, citizens, and activists alike petition for a path to citizenship for the millions of undocumented people who live among us and contribute to America's culture and economy. We have support. And knowing that we are fighting on the right side gives us hope. We can learn how to protect ourselves, know our rights (yes, we all—you included—have rights!), educate others, and fight strong and hard together.

Behind every one of the headlines on deportation there is a family. Parents. Innocent children. True stories that are rarely told. At last, I've found the courage to tell you mine.

To the left is my father's little apple (*manzanita*). My parents said I looked like a little apple when I was born. To the right is Diana, the nurse who helped deliver me.

Strike a pose!

Real fresh as a freshman in high school

I was just getting out of my Boyz II Men rehearsal.

1

NOT QUITE RIGHT

That bright spring day started off like any other. I know because I've replayed it in my head hundreds and hundreds of times, trying to make sense of it. Trying to piece together what happened.

"Diane, come eat your breakfast," came my mother's voice from the kitchen.

I was shoving books in my bag, hustling to get out the door. "I gotta go!" I yelled back, because—let's face it—I had 'tude.

"You've got another second," she said, following me down the hall. "You need to eat something."

"No, I *don't* have another second," I groaned. "Why do you always do this to me?" If there was one thing I disliked, it was being late. Especially when I was heading to a school I loved: the Boston Arts Academy (BAA). Before Mami could say another word or even hug me good-bye—*slam!*—I was out the door and off to class.

It was nice out, around seventy degrees. After a frosty winter, the weather was improving—and so, it seemed, was my family's luck. The day before, against all odds, my dad had a winning Powerball ticket. A few thousand bucks—and for us, it was the jackpot. On top of that, the love was flowing again in our house. Our family bonds felt close. A sign, perhaps, that better times were coming.

I peeped at my watch, mid sprint across campus. *Three minutes until the bell.* BAA, a performing arts high school in the heart of Boston, had truly become my home away from home. I could feel a prickle of energy as I approached. Even before 8:00 a.m., the place was buzzing. You know when cameras roll backstage on shows like *America's Got Talent* and *The Voice*? Well, that was the vibe (minus the cameras) of BAA. There'd be all these kids dancing around and stretching in the hallways. Next door, another group would be belting out songs or hanging their art up on the walls. The energy was epic, particularly right before spring fest—the one night our parents got to see us perform. It was the most special night of the year. And my song—a duet called "The Last Night of the World" from *Miss Saigon*—was part of the finale. My performance had to be better than good—it had to be Beyoncé-style *flawless*.

Right on time but a bit out of breath, I rounded the corner into humanities class. First, we had subjects like math and science, and then came the classes I lived for—theater, art, music.

Nine. Ten. Eleven. Noon. With each passing hour, I couldn't help noticing a weird feeling in the pit of my stomach. The kind you get when something isn't quite right. Maybe because I hadn't eaten breakfast. Maybe because I was nervous for the solo. Most likely, though, I figured it was because of how I'd treated my mom; I knew I needed to apologize.

Spring fest rehearsal came at the end of the school day. My teacher Mr. Stewart was already in the music room. So was Damien—the sweet black kid with a 'fro and glasses who was the other half of my duet.

"You need to warm up?" Mr. Stewart asked me from his perch at the piano. As usual, he was wearing a tie, a dress shirt, and that big grin we all knew him for.

"I'm cool," I said, stashing my backpack in a chair and hurrying over to them. Mr. Stewart played the ballad's opening notes. Damien's part was first.

"'In a place that won't let us feel,'" he sang softly. "'In a life where nothing seems real, I have found you . . . I have found you.'"

Next was my verse. "'In a world that's moving too fast,'" I chimed in a little off-key. "'In a world where nothing can last, I will hold you . . .'"

9

Mr. Stewart stopped playing. "You sure you're okay, Diane?" he asked.

I shrugged, a little embarrassed. I'd been practicing this song in my bedroom mirror and in the shower for days; I knew it up and down. "Just rusty," I told him.

"Let's try it again," Mr. Stewart said.

I stood up tall and cleared my throat. Closing my eyes helped me concentrate.

"'In a world that's moving too fast,'" I sang. "'In a world where nothing can last, I will hold you . . . I will hold you.'"

I opened my eyelids long enough to see my teacher nod. *Phew.* All year, I'd been trying to figure out whether this music thing was for me. Whether I could really make it as a singer. And thanks to Mr. Stewart, I was starting to believe I had a shot. I couldn't wait for my family to see me perform. The anticipation made me giddy.

On the way home from rehearsal, I stopped at Foot Locker. Earlier that morning, Papi had generously given me a crisp fifty-dollar bill from his Powerball win. "Buy yourself something nice, sweetheart," he told me. "Anything you want." I'd had my eye on this pair of classic Adidas shell-toes for weeks. Splurging on them was a no-brainer.

I proudly handed the cashier that shiny fifty-dollar bill. "You can wear them out of the store if you want," he said. I stuffed my old sneakers in my bag and headed off to the T—the Orange Line. It was five thirty. Definitely time to head home for dinner.

At six fifteen, the train pulled into the Stony Brook station. I strolled across the platform, careful to keep my Adidas fresh. They were so *dope*.

The sun was setting. I knew my parents would be wondering what time I'd get home. *I should let them know I'm on my way*, I thought. I spotted a pay phone—yes, pay phones were still a thing—dropped a quarter in, and dialed. *Ring. Ring. Ring. Ring.* "You've reached Maria, Hector, and Diane," said my mother's voice on the machine. "We're not here right now. Please leave us a message." *Beep.*

One of my parents was always home by this time. Always. Neither of them had mentioned having plans—then again, I'd bolted from the house that morning, maybe before they'd had a chance to tell me. That seemed unlikely, though. *Where could they be?* With trembling hands, I threw off my backpack and checked the pockets for quarters. Bingo. I forced the coin into the slot and pressed hard on each digit. *Ring. Ring. Ring.*

All at once, I jetted. I'd run these three blocks to our house dozens of times; I knew the route in my sleep. *Let them be home*, I prayed with every step. *God, please—let them be there. One block. One and a half. Two blocks.* A girl on her scooter called out, "Hey, Diane!" but I was sprinting too fast to answer.

When I made it onto our street, I saw my dad's Toyota station wagon in the driveway. Relief. *They didn't hear the phone*, I reassured myself. *They've gotta be here.* I rushed up to our porch and held my breath, bracing myself for what I'd find on the other side of that door.

Two-year-old me in Boston Common

Downtown Orlando, excited to go on this contraption

I thought I was Selena Quintanilla. I was not allowed to wear this outfit out.

2

WONDER YEARS

To make sense of my family's story, let's start at the beginning.

On July 21, 1986, I entered the world with a privilege that has shaped my entire existence. Because I was born in the United States, I received a gift guaranteed by the Fourteenth Amendment of our Constitution: citizenship. My mother and father—or Mami and Papi, as I lovingly call them—and my big brother, Eric, would've done just about anything to have that blessing for themselves, too.

Mami and Papi worked. And I mean superhard. That's what it takes to make it in America as you're struggling for citizenship. From the time they arrived from Colombia, they accepted the sort of low-paying jobs that make some people turn up their noses. Scrubbing toilets. Painting houses. Mowing lawns. Mopping floors. The kind of work no one else wants to do. The kind of work we sometimes don't even notice is being taken care of. My dad, Hector, left for his shift as a restaurant dishwasher well before sunrise; at noon, he went to his other job at a factory. Monday through Friday and sometimes on weekends, my father worked. It's how he made ends meet for us.

My mother, Maria, did everything from babysitting to cleaning hotels and office buildings. When I was small, she took me along for her shifts. As she wheeled her supply cart through the aisles, stopping to vacuum and wipe, she let me wander. "Put that back, Diane," she'd scold if she caught me touching things. Almost immediately, I'd be on to other mischief—swiveling in a chair and play typing, pretending I was a secretary. I could always entertain myself. My imagination came with me wherever we went.

My parents came here as immigrants to make sure I had opportunities that weren't available in Colombia. I often took it for granted that even though they had very little, didn't know the area, and didn't have the same technology we have today like smartphones, Yelp, or navigation, they still managed to find cool places to take me and my friends. I remember how they found a great skating rink they would take us to and watch while we had fun on the ice. I think about those days often, how they tried to give us the very best and help us live the most normal lives possible. When I think about skating in that rink I realize how much they sacrificed.

One of my favorite things to do when I was in elementary school was to find a spot on our sofa, curl up with the remote, and flip through my favorite shows. I also had this huge collection of Disney movies. I knew every character by heart, like Princess Jasmine, Belle, Simba, Cruella, and Pocahontas—yeah, they were my homies. By kindergarten, I'd become convinced I was Ariel from *The Little Mermaid*. I dressed like her, sang like her. And of course, I knew all the details of her wish to escape from her life to another. Ariel was my kind of girl—a dreamer.

"How does your song go?" my brother, Eric, teased me one Friday. "Is it 'Under the ocean'?"

"Shut up," I said, rolling my eyes, embarrassed. He'd overheard the rendition of "Wish I could be . . . part of that *w-o-o-o-rld*!" that I'd recently hollered into my microphone (and by microphone, I mean my mom's hairbrush).

Eric, who is ten years older, kept an eye on me when our parents were out. Can you imagine growing up with a sibling who's a full decade older? It's like being an only child. Think about it: When I was six, Eric was sixteen. Which means that, for the most part, he did his thing and I did mine.

He was cool, taking me along with him, always having my back. "Come on, baby girl," he'd say when we'd scrounged up enough loose change from beneath our couch cushions. "Let's go down to Chuck E. Cheese's." There, he'd play video games while I jumped myself silly in the inflatable bouncer. When we got home, we'd curl up in front of the tube again. When it came to TV hang time, Sundays were the best. Eric would mix up one of his chocolate shakes or fruit smoothies, and we would watch *The Simpsons*. It was our weekly tradition.

My parents started early and worked long hours, but they made sure that they usually finished work by dinnertime. Family meals were important to us. At five, the smell of Mami's rice and beans; fried plantains; and *sancocho*, a Colombian soup with corn and beef, wafted through our halls, rising to mix with the sound of salsa music. My mother and father are both fantastic cooks. Mami had her signature dishes, and Papi was always creating something new, sometimes adding an American, Chinese, Italian, or Dominican twist. One thing is for sure, our fridge was never empty. Papi would always say we didn't have much but at least we had food. I didn't ask for much, as long as he'd make me my favorite weekend snack of "*pulpos y papitas*" (octopus and fries). Papi would cut a hot dog in half and slice it in the middle two ways so the hot dog looked like it had tentacles, and when fried, the tentacles would come out looking like an octopus. My dad was always doing fun little things like that for me.

I was easy to please: I'd eat pretty much anything, as long as it had ketchup on it . . . and the foods didn't touch one another. "Ooh, that's delicious!" my mother would declare upon tasting her creation. Then as she prepared my plate, she'd pour the beans directly over the rice. "Mami!" I'd protest. "Can you please keep them separate?"

Dinner was our time to catch up. It was also my chance to take center stage. Once the family had gathered around the table, I'd belt out whatever Selena or Whitney Houston hit I'd just learned. "'And I . . . will always love you!'" I sang one evening, lifting an arm to add drama. My audience applauded as if I'd brought down the house at Madison Square Garden. "That's wonderful, honey!" Mami exclaimed. After a few more ballads, Papi would cut my concert short. "That's enough, *chibola*!" he'd say through laughs. He'd given me that sweet nickname after he'd heard it on a Peruvian TV show; it's slang for "my little girl." Whenever he said it, I cracked up.

We moved a lot, but all within a small area of Boston. If the rent went up, we searched for somewhere more affordable. Our homes were small, with tiny bedrooms. Eric usually had his own space, but until I was five, I slept with my parents. As I got older, Mami would create a makeshift bedroom for me, mattress and all, in the living room. Sometimes, we lived in an apartment; other times, we were in a two-family house. I didn't care, as long as we were together. We always made do with what we had.

My mother did all she could to make our surroundings

nice. She hung lacy curtains that she'd gotten on sale. She spruced up our bathroom with a blue fluffy floor mat. On her days off, she dusted and organized the living room. She had a thing for scented candles. During the Catholic holidays, she'd line up a row of them, lighting each to fill our living room with a sweet smell.

Mami took pride in how our home looked, and how she herself looked. She valued cleanliness as much as an honest day's work. She saved her pennies so she could occasionally splurge on lotion or lipstick; she kept her nails polished. And before bed, she brushed her dark, shoulder-length mane until it was silky.

Papi was well-groomed, too. His short hair was swept neatly back, his mustache perfectly trimmed. He wore cologne daily. No matter how much they struggled with money, they made sure Eric and I always rocked at least one cool outfit. They taught us to make the most of what we had and to look our best. They also passed on an important lesson—that our bond with each other and our neighbors was the greatest treasure of all.

In our community, we looked out for one another. When my parents' or our neighbors' friends fled here from Colombia, they often slept on our floor. "We need to help them get settled," Mami would explain as she scooted over my mattress to make room for the visitors. Just as my parents' friends and family had done for them, Mami and Papi would hook up newcomers with work, like cleaning or house painting. Show them where to get affordable groceries. Help them with English. Listen to their stories from home. Encourage them to get residence or citizenship that would allow them to live in the United States legally.

At home, and in the community, we all spoke a mix of Spanish and accented English. People with accents are often dismissed. It's assumed that they don't know the language well. The way I see it, though, an accent is a sign of hard work and bravery. Of stepping outside your comfort zone, learning a language that you weren't raised with. There's ambition in an accent, which I have always deeply admired.

Between my nightly performances and Los Hermanos Lebrón blaring from our radio, there was rarely a quiet moment. Did the noise annoy the people on our street? Not one bit. In immigrant communities all over the globe, celebrating is part of the culture. It's part of survival. When your relatives are thousands of miles away, you make up for it by connecting with those around you who speak your language. Eat your food. Love your music. Honor your traditions. We showed up for one another's barbecues, baptisms, anniversaries, *quinceañeras*. And Thanksgiving and Christmas? Off the chain. We partied our way from one home to the next.

Halloween was my favorite holiday. It was at a neighborhood get-together that I met two of my closest friends. I was five. Mami had recently befriended another Colombian lady,

Amelia, who lived nearby in Jamaica Plain. She was having a gathering, just because; Colombians don't need a reason to party. Mami brought me, and that weekend, I made my debut as Tinker Bell. Amelia's daughter, Gabriela, also five, was dressed as Snow White; her cousin, Dana, was Minnie Mouse. When a flying fairy, a lovely princess, and a polka-dot-clad mouse come face-to-face, there's zero need for small talk. That's why I cut to the chase: "Wanna dance?" I asked. Both girls nodded and grinned. After we'd shown one another our best moves, there was no looking back; I had two best friends for life.

The next Halloween, at a church costume contest, we expanded our BFF circle by one. "Nice tutu." I smirked at this girl named Sabrina, who'd shown up wearing the same white ballerina outfit I had on; I had a total "chick stole my look" moment . . . like come on, this girl is not going to out-ballerina me! We both bolted on that stage, full throttle. Thirty pliés, sautés, and whatever else we were trying to pass off as ballet later, we both lost the contest. Sabrina and I realized there was no other way to recover but to become besties.

"Mami," I'd beg after school, "can my friends come over?"

"They can if you've finished your homework," she'd say, cutting up a pepino cucumber ahead of supper.

My mother's answer was all it took to send me scurrying to round up the girls. Some days, I'd hang with Dana and Gabriela; other times, it was just me and Sabrina. But whenever all four of us got together, we were the ultimate #squadgoals. We Rollerbladed. We rode our bikes. We splashed in the public pool. But mostly, we lingered in the yard with our dolls so my parents could watch us. Every thirty minutes or so, I'd shuffle in to sweet-talk Papi into giving me Popsicles. "You're not going to be hungry for dinner!" Mami would say disapprovingly. As if that could stop me!

Sometimes, when the world is spinning too fast, I close my eyes and recall those afternoons. Papi, sticking his head out the screen door simply to check on me and my friends. Mami, stirring her stew while humming and swiveling her hips to the rhythm of *cumbia*. Us girls, lost in our laughter, disappearing into our world of dolls, books, board games, and imagination. Supper on the stove. Music in the air. Love all around. My wonder years.

This summer was lit. Right before my parents were deported.

Mami and Papi looking real '70s

3

MI FAMILIA

Some backstory about my family. Warning: love, loss, and homesickness ahead.

My mother and father loved Colombia. Moving to the United States was not their original plan. Mami, the fourth eldest of seven, was raised in Palmira—a country town in the Cauca River valley. The land is gorgeous, warmed by the tropical sun overhead. Linens hang from clotheslines. Farmers, with carts of fresh mangoes, plantains, avocados, and papayas, line the dirt road leading into the main square. Locals bike to and from their jobs as field-workers. Or as plant-workers. Civil servants. Fishermen. Maids and cooks for the wealthy. In the evenings, as dusk turns to darkness, families share their meals and stories. As impoverished as many Colombians are—nearly a third of residents live in poverty—they've maintained a spirit of optimism and strength.

My mother's parents clung to their hope. They lived without indoor toilets and electricity, basics many of us take for granted; yet they held on to their desire to give their kids opportunities. For three decades, they worked their fingers to the bone, harvesting sugarcane in the fields. They used their income on their kids' schooling. Two of my mother's siblings are college-educated. My uncle Pablo is a schoolteacher; my uncle Carlos trained as an industrial engineer. Yet in Colombia, going to college doesn't necessarily bring opportunity. Those who are born into power stay in power; those who are born into poverty stay impoverished. This can be true in America, too, but it is even more intense in Colombia, where there is far less money to go around. It doesn't matter how admirable one's work ethic or education is: For those who don't come from money, it's almost impossible to break into a new life.

Nonetheless, my brave mami, with her generous, outgoing spirit, set out to become a teacher at age seventeen. While completing her studies, she fell in love. She left school, married, and became pregnant. Then, during the first few months of her pregnancy, she made a crushing discovery: her "husband" was *already* married and had another family, one he'd hidden from her. Mami was completely shattered. Alone, she wept until, in August 1976, doctors delivered my brother. It was just Eric and my mom then.

My dear papi, who grew up a few streets over from Mami in Palmira, survived his own heartaches. He was fourteen when his father died suddenly of an aneurysm. Right then, the carefree joys of childhood flew out the window. Still coping with the tragedy, he was forced to find work to support his family. He, the seventh of eight children, began picking beans in the fields while he was still in school. More sadness followed. Several months after the funeral, Papi's mother tragically passed away in a bus accident. Now orphaned, my father had no choice but to set aside school altogether to work full-time in the fields. His siblings, my aunt Luceny and aunt Tenda, eventually became teachers; my uncle went on to work as a clerk. Like my mother, my father grew up with so little yet made the most of what he had.

My parents didn't know each other as children, despite living nearby. They met in their twenties. In those days, my mother's family was known in the neighborhood for throwing dance parties. My father went to one, where he noticed her shining smile. She was the best dancer in the room. By then, my father already had a reputation as an amazing salsa dancer. He was also cool. His sister, who'd been a seamstress, always made him fly outfits. Around town, people called him Chino Pinta, which is slang for "well-dressed." My mother already knew of him and had a crush from afar. He was as handsome as he was charming and reserved—a perfect balance for my mother's outgoing personality.

In a nation where safety and stability can feel out of reach, love made their lives more bearable, even sweeter. Together, they struggled along on their small paychecks. Papi worked from dawn until nightfall at a sugarcane plant, while Mami worked for a bus company called Palmira Express.

My parents had been with each other for only six months when Mami experienced more misfortune: Her younger sister was killed by random gunfire. Then, exactly one year later, my mother's mom suffered a heart attack. "Your grandmother died of a broken heart," my mother has often told me.

Those tragedies shook Mami to the core of her being. Her love for Eric and my father is what kept her going. She yearned to escape the despair all around her, though, to start over someplace else. She prayed her son, my brother, would have a better life. One that was free of the tragedies she and Papi had suffered.

An idea sparked in Mami's head. Years earlier, her older sister, Milena, had moved with her husband from Colombia to Passaic, New Jersey. They'd been granted permanent residence. Mami, who'd visited my aunt many times, saw opportunity there. And best of all, she saw a place far, far away from her painful losses.

"We should go stay with my sister and get on our feet," Mami told my father. At first, Papi, always careful, wasn't

27

convinced that going to America would help. But deep down, he couldn't help admitting that it was an intriguing idea. They desperately needed money and a fresh start. So, in 1981, with all their belongings stuffed into two suitcases, they arrived in New Jersey, on a visitor visa that would allow them to stay for ninety days. It was the kind of visa that was the easiest for them to get because they were invited and hosted by family members who were here legally.

My dad still had his doubts. My mother planned never to look back.

America wasn't initially the dreamland my parents thought it would be, though with the help of family and friends, they eventually hustled up some part-time jobs.

"Let's see if we can make it work," Mami told him. Though they had little money, it was far more than they could make in Colombia. Papi reluctantly agreed. But he was bothered by the fact that after those ninety days, they would be in the country without legal documents. He hated living with the fear that, without warning, they could be deported. If he had to leave, he wanted it to be by choice—not because he had been kicked out.

There was one thing they saw eye to eye on without question: Somehow, some way, they needed to get citizenship or legal permanent residence that would allow them to stay.

They'd grown to love this country and longed to call it their homeland.

One year stretched into five. They still had just enough cash to keep themselves fed and clothed. By 1986, they had what they've told me is their proudest accomplishment: me. Not much else had gone right for my parents, but—humble brag—I was right. One hundred percent.

I was tiny when our family moved from New Jersey to Boston. "You'll be able to find more work there," a friend had told Mami. "It's a great place to raise kids." In January 1987, on the eve of a big snowstorm, Papi loaded up everything we had and we set out for the four-hour drive. Ahead of the trip, my parents had managed to set aside a bit of savings. On the morning we moved into our apartment in Hyde Park, my father handed the landlord a neatly stacked set of bills, just about everything he had. At least our rent was covered—for the first month, anyway.

Like all families, mine has #drama. For starters, Eric and Papi did not get along, particularly once my brother reached adolescence. At the age of fifteen, Eric found himself in a dark place. It can feel impossible to dream big for yourself when you don't have the legal papers required to work or vote in the place you call home. Or when you are reduced to being "an illegal" in the minds of others. As smart as Eric is—he can kick it with the best of 'em at math and English—he lost interest in school. His grades slipped. He stayed out past curfew with his girlfriend, Gloria.

"Where were you last night?" Papi asked Eric one Sunday morning when my brother trudged into the kitchen. I, then seven, was eating a bowl of cereal. Mami and Papi were seated with me at the table.

Eric didn't look at my father. "None of your damn business," he mumbled. My mother and I traded a glance. Uh-oh.

It takes a lot to rile up my reserved father. My brother's behavior did the trick.

Papi stood and walked toward my brother until he was about three inches from his face. "You listen to me," he warned. "You don't curse in front of our daughter, you hear me?"

Eric shook his head, glaring. "You're not my father," he muttered. "I don't have to do what you say."

All at once, Papi grabbed Eric by his T-shirt. "You watch your mouth!" he shouted as the two stumbled from the stove to the fridge. "In this house, you're going to show some respect!"

Right then, Mami leaped from her chair and tried to wedge herself between them.

"That's enough!" she yelled. "Calm down!"

Eric stomped from the kitchen and into his bedroom, slamming his door so hard that the milk in my bowl swayed. I was too scared to speak or make a sound.

I didn't have the maturity or vocabulary to explain it back then, but I knew why my brother was unhappy. Eric was furious about the way his life was turning out. He'd been cheated out of having a birth father. While my parents showered me, their princess, with love, Eric felt like a misfit in his own family. My dad's intentions to protect us all were honorable, but he made his views clear: I was his baby girl; Eric was his stepchild.

Also, at the time, my parents didn't know how to address the mental health and behavioral issues that my brother faced, because in communities like the one we grew up in it wasn't something that was talked about or afforded. Mental health was a luxury.

Depression and anxiety are devastating burdens. There's so much pressure to be happy and bubbly and to keep your chin up. Reaching out and asking for help is brave. I wish we lived in a world where more people were given the support to do that.

Papi had his own sore spots. I could see how much he wanted to make a nice home for us—to make his risk of coming to America turn out to be worth it. He was also still recovering from the pains he'd experienced when he was Eric's age; I don't think you ever quite get over such devastation. Following his father's death, my dad had to become a grown-up overnight. The responsible one. He wanted to pass on a similar sense of responsibility to my brother and couldn't understand Eric's rebellion.

As for me, all I wanted was peace. That fight ended the way they all did: with my parents blaming each other. "You're babying Eric!" my father yelled at my mother that night. "Let him grow up!" There I sat, in my small rocking chair in our living room, watching helplessly. The fighting worsened until Mami, her face covered in tears, grabbed a box of buttons near her. She lifted her arm to hurl it in Dad's direction. The buttons—big ones, little ones, dozens of them in different colors and shapes—scattered across the floor.

"Stop it!" I screamed through sobs. "Stop it or I'll call the police!"

Silence fell over the room. My father slid down onto the couch near me. From her chair on the other side of the room, Mami gave me a blank look. For as long as I live, I will never forget what she said next.

"Go ahead and call the cops," she whispered, her voice raspy from the yelling. She paused. "Then they can come and send us all back to Colombia."

I gazed at her but couldn't bring myself to respond. My thoughts raced as I tried to make sense of what I'd just heard. Finally, I asked, "What are you talking about, Mami?" Tears stung my eyes, blurring my vision. "What do you mean, they'll send you back?"

She shifted forward in her chair and dropped her head. "I mean they'll deport us, Diane," she said. "They'll take us all away from you."

I stared at her, then over at my father, and then at Mami again. By this point, I already knew my parents' legal status. In fact, I don't recall a time when I *didn't* know they were undocumented. In our house, that was just understood. A fact of life. But at seven, I hadn't known what their status could mean for *me*. For the first time, I realized that with a single phone call, I could lose the most important people in the world to me.

After midnight, my parents kept arguing in their bedroom. I hated it when they fought; it made me so anxious. What if they never stopped fighting? What if they stopped speaking to each other and we never sat down to dinner all together again? What if they split up? Sadness weighed my heart.

In the dim light of my corner in the living room, I rose from my little mattress and turned on a lamp. At the foot of my bed lay my large nylon dress-up bag. My costumes were inside, a jumble of tiaras and bright metallic fabrics. I put on my princess getup, a pink gown. Mami's heels, the ones she wore to mass, sat near the couch. I slid in one bare foot at a time, wobbled a bit, then stood up straight. On this night, I would be Molly. Or Olivia. Or Taylor. Or Emma. Or any little white girl who had it easy. Whose parents never bickered. Whose brother didn't hurt. Whose family would never, in a million years, be pulled apart. There, in my land of make-believe, I could always find a happy ending.

Josie and the Pussycats. Thanks for never letting me get beat up.

My mother was afraid she'd never have another Christmas again, so she put every ornament possible on the tree and dressed me like an elf.

4

UNDERGROUND

When you're the child of undocumented immigrants, you learn to keep your mouth shut. Someone wants to know where your family is from? It's none of their friggin' business. You know how gossip works. We didn't want word to spread.

"*Nuestra situación no está resuelta,*" my father frequently told me. "Our situation isn't settled." The funny thing is that the fear of standing out for *not* being a citizen made him behave like a model citizen. Papi was careful out in the world, never saying anything that might suggest he was undocumented. The worst thing that could happen would be drawing the attention of the police or other authorities, and so he followed laws perfectly, never running yellow lights or speeding.

Our lives revolved around Mami and Papi's quest for

citizenship. They were constantly strategizing about how to get their papers. Or arguing about whether they ever would.

In 1986, the year I was born, the Immigration Reform and Control Act was passed. It allowed immigrants who'd entered the country illegally before 1982 to apply for amnesty, which is a pardon from the government. Mami saw it as an opportunity to finally get legal status.

"Let's file our papers," she pleaded with my father. Papi, ever the reluctant one, tried to talk her out of it, but Mami filed anyway. She was denied.

Dad later applied himself but was too scared to follow up with the process. He worried that if he gave his name and story to authorities, he'd be handcuffed and immediately deported for having overstayed that ninety-day visa. Yes, being granted amnesty could mean becoming legal residents in the country. But being rejected could mean being torn away from the family and thrown into prison. Like so many others around us, my dad just wanted to do the right thing, to keep us together.

In the spring of 1997, when I was almost eleven, a woman in the neighborhood gave Papi a tip. "I know a lawyer who can do all the paperwork for you," she told him, handing him the attorney's business card. "You should go see him. I've heard he's good. He's a Harvard Law School graduate."

That evening over supper, my father pulled the card from his wallet and slid it across the table toward Mami. He smiled. "I'm going to check out this guy tomorrow," he told her.

My mother was surprised. She picked up the card, turned it over a couple of times, and brought it right up to her face. She then lowered it and ran her fingertip across the gold-embossed lettering. "This looks good," she said. "How do you know this guy?"

"You know Betty, the Guatemalan woman at the end of the block?" he said. "She heard that this lawyer is helping people get their green cards."

My mother beamed. "Good," she said, setting aside the card to begin clearing the dishes. "Maybe Diane can go with you."

Everyone has a helpful job in a household, and this was Eric's and mine: translating English. Neither of my parents speaks English fluently. Not that they didn't try. In fact, my dad wanted to learn it so badly that, over the years, he took classes and practiced into the wee hours. But as a teenager, he'd lost hearing in his left ear while working in a sugarcane plant. Picking up the language was hard, and he was shy about speaking it. Mami's skills were stronger, but she didn't understand everything. Eric and I translated everything, from electric bills to ingredients on food packages. We accompanied my parents to medical appointments to explain to them what their doctors were saying. So for Papi's visit with the attorney, I'd definitely need to tag along. And besides, I was Papi's buddy. He took me almost everywhere.

On the Saturday of the appointment, we pulled into the lot of a towering office building in downtown Boston. Papi had on his nicest jacket, tie, and newly shined shoes; I wore a floral cotton dress and white sandals. "Stay close to me," Papi whispered as we made our way through the sliding-glass doors and into the lobby. "It's on the twelfth floor."

We emerged from the elevator into a long carpeted hall. Beneath fluorescent lights, we meandered down the corridor, scanning each door in search of the suite number. We passed an accounting firm. A dental practice. At the end of the hall-way was the law office. The attorney's name was engraved in all-capital gold letters across the door's placard. I don't remember the exact name, but it sounded all-American—something like Bradley Scott or Dylan Taylor. He definitely wasn't Latino.

We stepped inside. There sat a man in his forties behind a large oak desk covered in papers. He wore a three-piece suit and smiled. The top of his head was bald and shiny.

"It's Mr. Guerrero, right?" he said, shaking my father's hand. Then he motioned toward two chairs. "Have a seat, sir. *Bienvenido.*"

Phew—this man spoke some Spanish. Not *great* Spanish, I'd soon learn, but good enough to lighten my translation duties. "*Cuéntame tu historia,*" the lawyer said. "I need to hear your story."

Papi leaned forward in the chair. He peered over at a cheesy poster of Lady Justice on the wall; below it was the framed Harvard diploma. My dad then looked back at the man and cleared his throat. "Well," he said softly, "I left Colombia so I could earn more money for my family."

"How long have you been in the United States?" the man asked.

"Since 1981," Papi said.

"Have you ever applied for citizenship?"

My father shook his head.

"Do you have a family member who's a citizen?"

"Well, my daughter," Papi said, looking over at me. "And my daughter's mother has a sister here, but she's a resident, not a citizen."

The lawyer inhaled deeply. "Well then, we've got a lot of work to do," he said. "I'll need you to fill out this questionnaire." He reached for a maroon binder on the top corner of his desk, opened it, and removed a thick packet.

Papi flipped through it. "So how many months does it take to get a green card?" he asked.

The lawyer chuckled. "Mr. Guerrero," he said, "I'm afraid it's years, not months. For some of my clients, it takes ten years or longer—especially if there's no family member who has citizenship."

My jaw dropped. My dad stared. "Ten years?" he said.

"It can even be longer than that," the man said. "But you never know. You might be one of the lucky ones."

My father scowled. "*¿Cuánto cuesta?*" he asked. "How much does it cost?"

The man didn't seem too bothered by our shock. He shrugged. "That depends on how long your case takes. My rate is three hundred an hour."

Papi gasped, rising from his chair. "We don't have that kind of money—"

"But," the man interrupted. "I can set up a monthly payment plan. I've assisted many people in your predicament."

Papi didn't look convinced. "So what would I need to pay you?" he asked.

"We can start with seven hundred dollars," he said. "But why don't you go through these papers. I'm sure I can come up with a plan that fits your budget." We thanked the man and left.

Back at home, Mami rushed out to meet us when we turned into the driveway. "So," she said before we could get out of the car, "how did it go?" She was thrilled that Papi was making an effort to find a lawyer and was impatient to hear about it.

Papi sighed. "I'll have to find myself a third job."

She frowned for a moment. Then, always trying to be upbeat, she said, "Well, I could take on some extra babysitting. And we do have some savings."

"True," said Papi. "I'll have to see what I can work out with him."

I was in suspense. If this was our chance to get my parents permanent residency, could we make it work? That week, I had some new homework: tackling that packet. The following Sunday, when my dad and I returned to the lawyer's office, he seemed impressed that we'd pulled it together so quickly. "Very good, Mr. Guerrero," he said, flipping through the pages. "Now we can talk about the payment terms."

My father spoke firmly. "The best we can do is five hundred up front. That's the highest I can go."

I watched the man's face expectantly. He paused. "You've got yourself a deal, Mr. Guerrero," he agreed. My dad's face lit up. "I'll start your case tomorrow."

The two shook hands vigorously. On the way out, my father paid the attorney. "*Gracias,*" he said, holding back tears. "I appreciate this very much."

The whole way home, Papi kept glancing over at me but didn't speak. He didn't have to. We both knew what the meeting could mean for us. The route to citizenship came with setbacks, but at last we'd taken a step forward.

I always loved school, but I wasn't the best student. Maybe because I had the attention span of a goldfish. Getting A's in music and gym was easy, and I could sometimes swing a B in English. But when it came to math and science, I was doomed for summer school. My parents pushed me to do well; after all, part of the reason they'd come here was to give us a solid education. But they had their hands so full with working and keeping Eric on track that they couldn't give much attention to my homework, and tutors were too pricey. They recognized I was a good girl, that I took school seriously. So, given everything going on in our house, my average grades had to be sufficient.

"No cartoons until you're done with math," Papi would tell me. I'd sit there, fidgeting at our kitchen table, my mind wandering off to anything but multiplication tables. I envied those kids who could zip through their assignments. *Why can't I be like that?* I'd think. *Why can't I concentrate?* As hard as I tried, I could. Not. Seem. To. Focus. My family's in-limbo status didn't make that any easier.

My first school, Ohrenberger Elementary, was great. The campus was clean, the classes solid. Starting in kindergarten, Mami put me in bilingual classes. She wanted me to learn to read and write in both English and Spanish. I got a little of both languages, but I never felt like I was fully mastering either. I did, however, discover my first musical love: jazz. Around third grade, my chorus teacher played the class legends like Louis Armstrong, Billie Holiday, and Ella Fitzgerald. I was hooked from the opening note. I'd found my thing, which is good, because fractions certainly weren't it.

Elementary school at Ohrenberger was one thing; my

local middle school was another. Standardized test scores were often below the national average. There were too few teachers and too many students. The building was old and falling apart. There were seldom enough books or pencils to go around. Using her own money, my sixth-grade English teacher once purchased a batch of spiral notebooks. "Write out your vocabulary words in these tonight," she said, handing one to each of those who needed them. It wasn't that our parents wouldn't have bought them for us—it was that they couldn't afford to.

Sixth grade—ah yes, the year fights broke out. Kids disrupted class by throwing paper planes and pencils at teachers. Students turned up pregnant. And tensions erupted between rival gang members who'd show up to school with knives. I gotta say, the school was a hot mess. Dedicated teachers, administrators, and social workers worked around the clock to help students reach their academic potential. But they were fighting a tough battle. The issues that plagued our neighborhood didn't just stay in the neighborhood; they showed up in the hallways, in the classrooms, in the cafeteria.

Of course, plenty of kids, like me, wanted to excel. Looking back on it, I can see that many were discouraged. Their lives were difficult. When you have little opportunity or support, and struggle to keep food on the table, the American dream is far out of reach. My goal was to keep my head down and get through each day.

Luckily, my BFFs, Sabrina, Gabriela, and Dana, also attended. Following the final bell, the four of us would meet up and walk home. "Stick together," our mothers reminded us. "And steer clear of trouble." We knew the drill: We were supposed to have one another's backs if anything wild went down.

"Wanna come over to my place?" Sabrina asked as we strolled along the sidewalk. It was a Wednesday afternoon toward the end of my sixth-grade year.

"My mother's not gonna let me," I said. "I've got a ton of history."

"Yeah, me, too," Gabriela added. "I need to get home."

Just as we turned onto my street, these two Puerto Rican girls rolled up on their bikes. One had on Timbs and thick black eyeliner; the other wore booty shorts and had a tattoo of a cross on her chest. I recognized them from campus. The one in the shorts glared at me.

"What's up, wetback?" she sneered.

I took a step back. So did Sabrina and Dana. Gabriela didn't budge. Of the four of us, she'd always been the tough one who tolerated zero garbage.

"Dude, why don't you leave her alone?" she snapped, taking the lead. "You don't even know us."

"Shut your mouth!" spat the girl. "All three of you need to take your flat, ugly faces back to Colombia!"

My heart was slamming in my chest. All at once, I hauled

off down the street, the blood coursing through my veins as I sprinted. "Let's get outta here!" I shouted. My hands shook as I clutched onto the padded straps of my backpack. TBH: I've always been a bit of a wimp. I didn't know what they wanted with us, but I wasn't about to stick around and find out. Sabrina, Dana, and Gabriela were right on my heels. We didn't stop to look back until we'd reached my front door. Thankfully, the mean girls had vanished.

"We can't let them scare us," said Gabriela, out of breath. But I was already shaken up. Once inside, I didn't tell my mother what happened. Instead, I buried my head in my homework, doing my best to forget.

That wasn't the first time we'd been bullied. In our area, which was mostly filled with Puerto Ricans and Dominicans, anybody who wasn't in one of those two groups was usually considered a "dirty immigrant." We were spat on. Cursed at. Looked down upon. And perceived as unattractive because of our native Indian features. I know, I know: Other Latino groups look similar. That goes to show how stupid discrimination is. And that the stigma of being undocumented exists even within the Latin community.

For the remainder of that year, whenever I spotted the two girls in the cafeteria, I ducked out and avoided eye contact. Rule *número uno* in my neighborhood: The best way to win a fight was to avoid it in the first place.

As tough as my middle school was, it did have one major

thing going for it—extracurricular activities. You name it, I was involved. In fifth grade, I joined the basketball team and chorus. In sixth, I became a cheerleader. In seventh, I signed up for the peer leadership program. I, along with a group of others chosen, attended training sessions on topics such as drug prevention and safe sex. Once a week, we then went around and talked to our classmates about how they could protect themselves. I loved it. For the first time, I felt useful, like I had a voice. A contribution to make. Something that set me apart from the bullies with nothing better to do.

For most of my childhood, I looked on helplessly as Eric struggled with depression, locking himself in his room. We didn't have the cash to send him to a therapist or counselor. Truth is, emotional wellness was something we—and many others in our community—couldn't afford to think about, no matter how much we struggled with it.

A year after leaving school, Eric discovered that he and his longtime girlfriend were expecting a baby. This news didn't go over so well with either of their families.

Did I mention our quarters were cramped? Well, Gloria moved in with us a few months into her pregnancy. Five people in a two-bedroom gets crowded. And tense. Which led to more arguing between Eric and my parents, and between Eric and Gloria.

But by June 1996, the newest member of our family

arrived. Eric drove home in his Toyota with Gloria and their sweet newborn. The whole way, my brother could hardly keep his eyes on the road as he glanced over his shoulder to check on his princess in the back seat. When the car pulled into the driveway, Mami and I hurried out front. The baby, wrapped in a soft pink blanket, had her lids tightly shut.

"What's her name?" I asked, peeking over the carrier's edge.

"It's Erica," Eric told me. He leaned down and pecked her on the forehead, which made her stir a bit and open her eyes. "Isn't she cute?"

I nodded, unable to stop grinning. She looked like a living doll. Rosy cheeks. Tiny toes. A bald head. She was the most beautiful baby I'd ever seen.

In the months following Erica's birth, Eric stepped up like never before. Fatherhood motivated him. He landed work, painting houses and mowing lawns. Rather than hanging out late with his buddies, he spent time with Gloria and the baby. In fact, their relationship began going well enough that they decided to marry. Soon after, Gloria began filing the papers to sponsor Eric for citizenship. With a green card, my brother could look for a job with benefits and a better income.

Or at least that was the plan. But his old behaviors returned. Maybe it was the blues. Maybe it was the difficulty of providing for his family. On the evenings when he was home, he and Gloria fought constantly. "I need you to help out more with the baby!" I once overheard her telling him. "And where were you last night?" Their marriage became so rocky that Gloria and Erica went to live with her parents in Hyde Park.

At that point, my brother went from sad to broken. He barricaded himself in his room. When he did drag himself out to go to the fridge, he and Papi got into it; as usual, Mami tried to be a peacemaker.

Me? I just sank deeper into fantasies about a life far away from the friction. Deep down, I wanted to be like teenagers on TV. Their biggest "problems" were whether they'd get asked to the prom, not whether they'd be jumped by haters or have their brother and parents deported. I wanted to be a "normal" child.

The idea of "normal" for me was embodied by the snazzy towns like Wellesley or Newton that Papi would sometimes drive us through on his days off. They looked like they were on a different planet than the one I came from. As we weaved our way through the ivy-covered houses, I'd stare from the car windows, imagining what it must be like inside. A child in Wellesley surely couldn't have the same problems as I did. If you were white and wealthy and impeccably manicured, your life had to be perfect, right?

The people inside were probably quiet and dainty, too, I figured. "Mami, stop being so loud! White people aren't loud," I'd hiss at her if she was laughing too loudly in the street. The hilarious thing is, I had no idea what white people did or didn't do—or, for that matter, how *anyone* lived behind closed doors. And Lord knows, loud folks come in all colors. But in the culture I was raised in, amid the countless media images I took in as a girl, I got this crazy notion that being white and well-heeled and educated made one *better*.

In the hours before sunup, as Papi prepared for his first shift, I lay awake on my bed, imagining a magical future that was a universe away from my own. Sometimes I'd imagine us in a house in Wellesley. Not even the biggest or most charming house; just a little house that was all ours. But even more than that, my fantasies took place onstage. Closing my eyes, I'd imagine a crowd roaring with applause. A lush velvet curtain rising. A golden spotlight shining down on my beaming face.

The older I got, though, the more I noticed that the performers who were in starring roles were . . . not Latina. In fact, I didn't see myself or my experiences *anywhere* in pop culture—not on TV, or in movies or in books. And that hurt. It suggested that other people's looks and experiences were more important to show than mine; that mine were somehow inferior, less deserving of attention and respect. Could a brown girl from an immigrant family ever be center stage? I wondered. Only one in a million girls reaches a dream like that, but in some small corner of my soul, I secretly nurtured the feeling that *I* could be that girl. Sometimes I felt all the self-confidence in the world. Other times I felt like I was crazy for even daring to daydream.

My mother was an early believer in me. "You're a shining star!" she'd proclaim each time I serenaded her and my dad. When I was a little girl, Mami's encouragement made me blush and giggle. But starting at around twelve, my response shifted. For some reason, her words began to sting. "You don't know anything!" I burst out one night after she'd announced I was destined for Hollywood. "Stop saying that!" My mother, stunned by my reaction, just stared at me.

Mami hadn't changed; it was me who was shifting. I yearned to perform, to find my way into the limelight. And yet the likelihood of that happening felt so small. *Like, I'm talented, sure. But look where we are, how we have to live.* Besides that, I could probably count on one hand how many Latinas were on TV. Of *course* I'm not going to "make it." So I placed a tight lid over the top of my dreams and hid them away. But, like fireflies, their light still burned inside me.

My first Communion, laughing at Gaby's imitation of one of the church ladies urging us to blow out our Communion candles. *(Apaguen la luz, apaguen la luz.)*

Dad and I rocking our pigtails and mustache in Palmira, Colombia

5

THE GOOD GIRL

I am a daddy's girl. Through and through. Mami and I are tight, but Papi and I have always had this connection. Our senses of humor can be really silly and playful. We can both be a little on the shy side. And we're both ultrasensitive. I'd catch him tearing up during one of those World Vision commercials with the starving children in it. When anyone saw him dabbing his eyes, he'd say he had a cold—but his "sniffles" were tears. He's almost as easily moved as I am—which is saying a lot, since I cry over literally anything and everything.

In the evenings, when my dad came through the front door, we had our own ritual: "Come here, *mi amorcito*," he'd say, with a big hug. "How was your day?" I remember how he smelled after work—like a factory. I liked the scent; probably because it meant Papi was close by, keeping me cozy and safe. On the occasional weekend when my father was off, he'd take me down the street to get ice cream. With my vanilla cone dripping under the sun's heat, we'd walk together to the park or library. Even as I edged toward adolescence, and most of my friends stopped wanting to hang out with their folks, I hung out with my papi.

My favorite adventure was going to the coast. We'd get up early, pack some snacks, load up our station wagon, and drive to Nantasket Beach. Some weekends, Mami joined or I'd invite my friends; other times, it was Papi and me. We'd hit the promenade and wander toward the Paragon Carousel. I'd grown a few inches, but he'd nonetheless hoist me onto the back of a horse and stand at my side as I spun around in delight.

Down by the shore, we'd build sand castles and watch the waves wash them away. "Papi, come in the water!" I'd plead. "Not today," he'd say; he couldn't get water in his damaged ear. "Please!" I'd beg; if I persisted, he'd pull some cotton balls from his pocket, stuff them into his ear canals. "I'll stay in for a sec," he'd tell me—but twenty minutes later, we'd still be splashing and laughing our heads off.

Upon returning home, my mother would wash sand from my hair and set out fresh clothes for me. Papi, worn out from our adventure, would doze off on the couch as Mami brushed my hair a million times to get out the tangles. "Wake up, *mijo*," she'd whisper to my dad when the sun had gone down. "Time for bed." Before going to his room, Papi would lean down and put his forehead against mine. I'd raise my chin so he could tickle my neck with his stubble. "Good night, little girl," he'd whisper. "Now it's time to sleep. *Es la hora de dormir.*" It was the kind of day I wished could go on forever. No tension between my parents. No drama or fighting about Eric. Just pure joy.

Papi and Mami made every celebration special—and Lord knows we had a lot of them. Birthdays were huge in our house. Friends, family, food, decorations—the works. For my tenth, we had a luau. The house was filled with flamingos, grass skirts, and lots and lots of pineapple. Of course my besties were there—Sabrina, Dana, and Gabriela. It was everything! My father came in with my birthday cake. My face lit up as brightly as the flickering candles on top. "Make a wish!" he urged, standing over me with his camera. I drew in a breath. My wish never changed from year to year. I prayed that my family would never be separated (and, of course, that I really would one day become a star), and blew out the flames.

As summer gave way to autumn and stretched into winter, Papi decked our halls with twinkling white lights and a pine tree that would make our home smell green and fresh. "Have you been naughty or nice this year, *chibola*?" he'd ask teasingly as he balanced the glistening star on the tree's top branch.

"Nice!" I'd yell, laughing. In the days leading up to Christmas, we gathered with other families to observe La Novena, a Colombian-Catholic holiday. As is tradition, we made our way from one house to the next through a winter wonderland, caroling and rejoicing. Bundling up was key in the chill Massachusetts air. I stuck close to Papi's side.

"You okay, hon?" he'd check in on me.

"I'm good," I'd reassure him. Our breath was so cold that it clouded in front of our mouths as we spoke. When we went indoors, into the warmth, my dad and I stood hand in hand as neighbors recited Scriptures and sang along to the sweet *villancicos* of "Mi Burrito Sabanero" and "Tutaina." There, swaying in our friends' living room and clenching my father's palm, I knew for sure I was cherished. I still know it.

My papi. My haven. My anchor. The caretaker whose arms I rested in, whose shoulder I leaned on. The father who worked so tirelessly before the sun even came out, to provide me with a childhood that was far happier than his own.

My parents raised me Catholic. Sunday school and mass every week. The rosary. The holy water. The Ten Commandments. Confession. They weren't super-religious themselves, but they wanted to give me a solid spiritual grounding, to teach me how to be honest, generous, and good. I completely embraced it. By middle school, I'd taken the whole Good Catholic Girl thing to its highest level.

Caught in the middle of a turbulent household, I held on to my Catholicism. The guidelines of religion were my anchor. Something to focus on. Something steady and unchanging. No matter how heated the arguments got, no matter how unstable my family's situation seemed, I could always light a candle or review the catechism. I was convinced Catholicism was the answer to every problem, the one sure way to bring good things into my life.

Papi frequently checked me when I misbehaved. "Be careful how you talk to your mother," he'd say if I'd snapped at her. "God is always watching." The heavenly father was our great protector, but he was also the ultimate judge—one whose punishment I feared deeply. I envisioned him sitting up in heaven on his throne, scanning the earth below with an all-powerful eye. He knew who'd been good and who'd been unkind, and he kept track. Anyone who disobeyed his commands or refused to repent would end up in hell.

Starting when I was in second grade, I became obsessed with repenting. If I, say, rolled my eyes at my teacher, I'd rush home, lock the bathroom door, cry, and then slap myself or pull my hair. I know that sounds weird and harmful, but I was under the impression that I deserved it. This was my way of doling out punishment on myself before God could step in and do it.

At age ten, I began preparing for my first Holy Communion—a huge deal among Latino Catholics. There were classes to complete. Verses to memorize. Prayers to recite. On the Sunday when I officially committed to the faith and accepted God into my life, I dressed from head to toe in white. I felt a mix of shyness and pride standing there in front of the congregation. I'd been baptized and confirmed. I'd received the body of Christ (the bread) and the blood of Christ (the grape juice). At the time, I thought it was wine. "I'm so drunk," I'd whisper to my friends as I stumbled back to the pew and we all giggled quietly. Afterward, at home, friends and neighbors gathered for a special dinner hosted by Mami and Papi. People gave me gifts and flowers. From then on, it was me, God, the Virgin Mary, and Saint Anthony—I did everything in my power to make sure the four of us stayed tight.

I prayed daily. On my bed in the evenings, I'd pull out a small flashlight and look through my little New Testament that Mami had brought for me. After reading a few passages, I'd then squeeze my eyes shut tight and ask God to keep my family safe.

After murmuring my favorite Hail Mary prayer, I'd make my usual requests. A little house, any house, one we could at last call our own. Citizenship for Mami, Papi, and Eric. That I would one day become a star. And, of course, that we'd stay together forever. If I sought God fervently enough, if I lived according to his principles and never strayed, he would reward my faithfulness by protecting my family. I believed that with all my heart. Every Good Catholic Girl does.

Papi continued paying the attorney each month. "Things are looking good," the man told my father. "We're getting closer."

My mother was starting to get antsy. "What's taking so long?" she'd press, shaking her head in annoyance. "We've been handing over money for months!" "Just be patient," Papi told her. "It'll happen." Mami tried to hold her tongue about it, but she was stressed. Enough with the waiting, she thought. It was time to try something else.

Now let's rewind for a minute: Before we left for Boston that snowy night when I was little, back when my parents were still living in New Jersey, Mami had spoken to an immigration lawyer. The lawyer had promised to help her get a green card, the golden ticket to permanent residency. So she submitted legal papers, which the lawyer would submit to the federal government—but upon our move to Boston, Mami halted the process. "I should reopen the case," she told Papi. "By the time you get your green card," she continued, explaining her reasoning, "I'll also be close to having mine."

In the fall of 1997, Mami got in touch with that lawyer in New Jersey, who pulled her file. "We still have your paperwork," the lawyer told Mami, "but it was never actually submitted to Immigration. You'll just have to give us some updates, and then we can get started on your case again." When Mami told Papi, he didn't like the sound of it.

"That was years ago that you filed those papers," he told her. "There's a whole new staff there now. How do they even know what was or wasn't already submitted? And why don't you just sit tight until I'm done with my papers, and then we can look into it?" But Mami was ready for a change, even if it meant taking a risk—so she forged ahead.

On an afternoon during spring semester of sixth grade, I came home ready to hit the books. Lily, one of Mami's closest friends in the area, had stopped in to see her. The two were talking in the kitchen as Mami prepared dinner for the evening.

"The strangest thing happened yesterday," Mami told her.

"What?" said Lily.

"I heard someone knocking on our back window," she said.

"Who was it?"

"I peeked through the blinds," Mami said, "but I didn't get a good look at him. Then he came around and knocked on the door."

"Did you open it?"

"Of course not," she said. "I just yelled out, 'Who is it?'"

"What'd he say?"

"He goes, 'Ma'am, I'm here from your utilities company.

We're just checking things out.' When I didn't respond, he went away."

"Did you call for someone?" asked Lily.

"That's the thing," Mami said. "I didn't. And no one called to tell me someone would be stopping by."

Lily was quiet for a moment. "I'm sure it was nothing," she finally said. "He was probably just checking your meters in the back of the house." Mami nodded. And just like that, she dropped it.

Our school fair was three weeks later. I needed to get my science project to class in one piece, so Mami agreed to drive me to school. She dropped me off at around 8:30 a.m. and tried to kiss me before I got out. "Mami, not here!" I rolled my eyes and pulled away. I'd reached that age when I didn't want to be seen kissing my mother in public. "I hope it goes well today," she said kindly, despite my outburst. "I'll be thinking of you."

The project was a hit with my teachers. I'd tested the hypothesis that aspirin makes plants healthy and strong by growing two potted evergreens—one with aspirin water added, the other without it. The first was the clear winner. Its plentiful leaves were a deep green compared with the yellowish leaves of the other. "Good job, Diane," my science teacher congratulated me. I grinned. *Wait until Mom hears*, I thought, heading home. She'd helped me with the project.

As I bounded up to our front door, my eyebrows furrowed. Something was off. For one thing, the door was cracked. For another, Eric was peeking out of it. He opened it, pulled me inside, and slammed it shut.

"What's going on?" I said. There was Mami's friend Lily, sitting on the sofa. Her eyes were red. She and Eric glanced at each other before he answered me.

"It's Mami," he said. He paused.

"What happened?" I asked, looking back and forth between them. "Where's Mami?"

"She's gone," he said crisply. He looked down at the floor.

I gazed at him. "*Gone?*" I repeated. "What do you mean *gone?*" I dropped my backpack at my feet. My palms trembled. My lips quivered. "Is she dead?" I asked.

"No, no, no," Eric said, shaking his head. "She's not dead. Immigration came and took her."

What?

There was a ringing in my ears. It sounded far away and close at the same time. The room in front of me blurred, and my head felt light. I couldn't feel my feet beneath me. Was I in a horror movie?

"Are you even listening to me?" snapped Eric. His words jolted me back to the present. "Our mother is about to be deported. She's been locked up."

He re-explained what he'd been saying a moment ago, that after Mami had dropped me off at school, she'd gone home and then headed to her cleaning job. She picked up some groceries for dinner that night. She'd agreed to drive Eric to and from an appointment that afternoon. Then, just as she was turning back onto our block, a policeman pulled her over.

And he was no ordinary cop; he was an immigration officer—the same man Mami had noticed creeping around our house. He asked her to step out and put her hands up. "We have a warrant for your arrest, ma'am," he told her, slapping handcuffs over her wrists. "You have the right to remain silent. Anything you say can and will be used against you in a court of law." Eric sat stunned and shivering in the front passenger seat. What could he do? If he jumped out, he too might be arrested. Besides, he didn't want to get Mami in worse trouble. The officials didn't even question him. They just took Mami away, and a moment later Eric got into the driver's seat and pulled the car into our driveway. He called Papi and told him to rush home from work. Then he called Lily.

As I was processing Eric's words, Papi stormed through the door. He flung down his lunch box and shouted, "What happened?" Every bit of life drained from Papi's cheeks as he listened to Eric. By the end of the story, he was crying.

There are few things scarier than when adults, your protectors, the ones who make you feel better, are afraid, too. Seeing the fear in Papi's eyes made me crumple. I hurled myself down onto the kitchen floor, heaving with sobs. Lily got down on the floor next to me and rubbed my back. "It's okay," she consoled. "Everything will be fine." At this, I cried even louder.

Papi went into his bedroom to think about what to do next. When he emerged, he told me something similar. "We'll get through this." But his eyes and behavior gave a different message. With every fiber in me, I knew he was as terrified as I was—maybe even more.

Later, in hushed tones in the kitchen, he and Lily talked. They thought they were whispering low enough to keep me from hearing. They were wrong.

"What do you think we should do?" Papi asked desperately. "Should we go to Jersey—and what if they come back for me tonight?" That question seized my heart. What would happen to me if *both* my parents were taken?

"They might return," Lily sighed. "They know where you are now, and—"

Papi interrupted. "But if they'd intended to arrest me, they would've done that this time."

Lily shook her head. "You probably shouldn't stay here. It may not be safe."

But we did stay. My father's theory about why this had happened was this: Mami put herself on the ICE's radar when she'd restarted that paperwork. Although the agency claimed her paperwork had never been submitted to the federal government, perhaps it *had* been. If so, then Mami had probably been followed by the authorities for weeks. They had just been waiting to pounce. But as long as he, Eric, and I lay low, he figured they would leave us alone. Besides, Papi had just made a double payment to the attorney. We couldn't afford to move.

None of us slept a wink that night. Nor the next. Nor the one after that. "*Padre Nuestro*," I'd whisper to God as I lay awake on my bed, "please help us." Desperately, I recited every prayer and Scripture I'd ever memorized. I couldn't help wondering if what was happening to my family was *my* fault. I racked my brain—what might I have done to bring the Lord's wrath on us? I'd given Mami attitude that morning. Could that have been it? Or had I committed some other sin I hadn't repented for? From dusk until dawn, the sounds in the neighborhood jolted me. A barking dog. A passing car. An alarm going off in the neighbor's house upstairs. With every shadow across the walls, with every key in the door, I feared that the officers had returned for the rest of us.

I had no teeth, but I was a great makeup artist. Me and Mama.

I had a 104° fever but still had time for a Kodak photoshoot.

6

WITHOUT MAMI

"I pledge allegiance, to the flag, of the United States of America," my classmates intoned. I loved reciting the Pledge of Allegiance; I was usually the first on my feet to do it. But this morning, I mouthed along zombielike, my head on another planet. My teacher noticed.

"Everything okay, Diane?" he asked.

"Oh, I'm fine," I said, avoiding eye contact. "Just tired." Thoughts of my mother blazed through my mind, but I vowed not to tell a soul that she had been taken. Only my best friends knew, and frankly, if I could've hidden it from them, I would have. That's how mortified I was.

The day after her arrest, Mami phoned home. From Papi's side of the conversation, I pieced together the details. She'd already been taken to a women's prison in New Hampshire, and within weeks she'd be deported from there. "Yes, we thought about moving," Papi told her. "But I don't think they'll return. And besides that, I don't really have the money to move right now."

I was surprised to hear them talking so openly since Mami was on a prison phone. Couldn't someone be listening in? Toward the end of the call, Papi handed me the phone. "Your mother wants to talk to you," he said. I took the receiver. My heart pounded in my chest.

Before Mami could say a word, I began to sob. "It's okay, Diane," Mami said. "You're going to be fine. Your father is taking care of everything. I just have to go away to Colombia for a while."

Why does everyone keep telling me it's fine? I understood that she, my dad, and Lily were all just trying to make me feel better. But clearly things *weren't* okay, and we didn't know what would come next. I could see right through their words of comfort.

"Diane?" Mami said. "Why don't you come to Colombia with me?"

I froze. I'd never even considered the idea of a life away from Boston. Away from America, the only country I'd ever lived in. I'd grown up hearing about my parents' homeland. But it was a world far, far away. And I couldn't bear the thought of leaving my father and brother alone, without me there to referee. My mind raced with reasons not to leave.

"No, Mami," I said, my voice shaking. "I can't. I have to stay here."

The line went dead silent. "Take care of yourself, honey," Mami finally said. "I love you. I'll see you again when I can."

In the following days, as I watched Papi slide from shock into despair, one thing became clear: Papi blamed Mami for her arrest. Behind his closed bedroom door, I heard him argue with her nightly over the phone. Why did she need to go sniffing around for those papers? he'd ask angrily. Why hadn't she listened to him? And why did she have to go around being the neighborhood socialite, letting anyone and everyone know our business?

"You're too open," he told her. "Just too friendly. Maybe it was that stupid paperwork that got you caught—but it also could've been someone around here who secretly wanted to take us down." Those were harsh words, especially for a woman sitting in prison. My dad didn't mean to be cruel. We were in crisis mode. Panic and confusion came spewing out like toxic sewage.

After Mami's deportation, Eric and my father fought nonstop. The arguments nearly turned violent a couple of times. "Stop it!" I'd scream, wedging myself between them, picking up where Mami had left off. I would try to distract them by making myself look crazy by screaming and pulling my hair, just like I did when I punished myself for being a "bad" girl. I felt out of control and in way over my head.

All I wanted was to finish up the school year and keep the truth hidden from my classmates. I tried to talk to Eric a few times, but he was just as overcome with grief as I was. His way of showing it was to cause trouble. My way of showing it was to disappear into my fantasy worlds, into my television shows, into my music, into my Bible. Into anything that would temporarily make me forget our sorrows.

My usually joyful relationship with Papi had gone quiet. In fact, we barely talked. Other than the same old "You cannot tell anyone what's going on"—and my answer of "I get it, Dad." In between his wars with Eric and his endless, exhausting hours at work, he sat hunched over the couch and stared blankly at the television. He was physically there but emotionally far away.

Mami called frequently from Colombia. "I miss you so much, Diane," she'd tell me over and over. "You should come here. We could start over. Things are a little better here now than they were before. We could get you into school."

But every time she brought up moving me to Colombia, my neck became extremely hot. "Instead of asking me to move there," I told her one evening, "you need to come *here*."

"I wish I could," she told me. "I would do anything to go back. But it's impossible right now."

I knew that was true. But while she was setting up her new life there, I couldn't help but be angry that I was in charge of keeping World War III from breaking out in our house. I was like, *Are you kidding me right now? My life sucks without you, and if I have to deal with these yelling dudes one more day, I am going to explode.* That didn't stop her from bringing up the idea of my going there. It got to the point that, whenever she called, I told my father to pretend I was asleep. I just couldn't bear to listen to it anymore.

No one had prepared me for this. I'd always known there was a possibility that one or both of my parents would be taken, but what was the plan? "You have to be strong," Papi would always tell me. I got that part. But what would happen *after* I flexed my emotional muscles? Where would I go? Would child services pick me up? What *were* child services, anyway? Would I go back to Colombia with one or both of them? There were no straightforward answers.

I didn't feel like talking or eating. Dad would offer me rice and beans in the evenings, and I'd push aside the plate. Every night in bed, I was haunted by the same question: *Did I do something to cause this? Did I displease you, Heavenly Father?* I'd tried to be so obedient. I'd followed the rules. And yet God had allowed the very thing I dreaded to happen. And I didn't understand why.

Two months passed. To my complete and utter surprise, Papi came home one night with big news. "Your mother's coming back," he told me.

"What?" I asked, bewildered.

"She found a way to get back into the country," he said blankly.

"But *how*?"

"I don't know all the details," he said in a way that told me there was more to the story than he was sharing. "She'll be here tomorrow."

Tomorrow? Jaw drop. A flood of questions filled my head. *How could she have found a way to get back into the States? Was that paperwork somehow sorted out? What aren't they telling me?*

Papi didn't seem thrilled. He seemed worried. Which made me worried, too. It's not that I wasn't happy Mami was returning, but I feared that it could put us all in danger of being arrested.

The next evening around seven, Mami pulled up in front of our house in a taxicab; Papi and I rushed out into the driveway to meet her. "My princess!" she said, dropping her suitcase to hug me. "Oh my goodness, it's so good to see you both!"

Mami didn't look like she'd just been through a horrifying ordeal. To my surprise, her smile was broad. Her clothes were cute. Her energy seemed open. I'd imagined she'd be undercover, maybe in a hat and glasses, or army fatigues like a secret agent. Neither Mami nor Papi told me the specifics of how she managed to get back across the border. To this day, I still don't know for sure. But I did know that only a mother who refused to be torn apart from her family would take the big risk of returning.

The plan was to move. Immediately. With Mami back, staying put was out of the question. My parents began making plans to go to New Jersey. We wouldn't stay with my aunt and uncle—the authorities might find us there. Instead, we'd find an apartment a few towns over. For a moment things seemed like they were about to come together for us. I gulped back the sadness of leaving Boston with the hope that in New Jersey, we'd all be together.

Until the day that, one week after Mami's return, she was arrested. Again.

That morning, my mother had been walking a couple of our neighbors' children to school—a side job she'd done for years. Single mothers who needed to get to work early would bring their little ones to our place before school. Mami would feed them breakfast and walk them to class. When I came home that afternoon, Mami's friend Lily was in our living room. Same spot. Same red eyes. Same look of exasperation. It had happened again, and *fast*. We couldn't believe it. Papi had no words.

When the ICE officer pulled up alongside her on the street and got out of the car, Mami began to cry; she knew what was coming. "Ma'am, we're going to need you to come with us," the officer told her. He placed her in handcuffs as another officer gathered the children. I'm not sure how or when the mothers received word that their children were being held at a local ICE facility. Whenever they did, Lily rushed to pick up her son, who was in the group. She then called my school and requested that they send me home immediately. When I walked through the front door, filled with dread that the worst had indeed happened, Lily was there waiting.

"She's gone," Lily said, pulling me into her arms. "Your mother has been arrested again."

Because we'd already been through this before, this news was both completely shocking and completely unshocking. It felt almost ridiculous, like, was this *really* happening to us? How could my mother be taken not once but *twice*?

Following this arrest, Papi wasn't taking any chances. "We're moving. We've gotta get out of here," he said. So we rented the tiny basement apartment of my parents' friend Olivia. She lived upstairs. The place was so small that we had to get rid of most of our stuff, and Dad put my little mattress on the floor in his room, next to his bed. Eric didn't join us. He had chosen to move to New Jersey and try to start over there. I missed him, but I also knew it was better for him and Papi to have a break from each other.

I wasn't expecting the Ritz, but this basement was scary. The ceilings were low. Dozens of boxes and storage bins lined the entrance. It smelled musky and moldy. The walls were crawling—and I mean *crawling*—with the biggest friggin' rats in the world. *Ugh.*

Papi worked even longer hours than before; he was sending my mother money in Colombia, on top of supporting us. In our dingy apartment, it was as if there was no distinction between a Monday or a Tuesday or a Friday. They all went like this: Papi got up. Left for work. Dropped me off with the neighbors upstairs, who gave me breakfast and sent me off to school. I'd sleepwalk my way through the day, and then watch *Peanuts* on Olivia's couch. For whatever reason, Charlie Brown was a source of comfort. I'd sit there eating endless Cheez-Its, one cracker after another, while peering at the screen. I was just passing time until Papi came home around six.

I think both of us were secretly hoping she'd magically reappear, as she had before. But months came and went, and summer stretched into fall. No Mami.

In school, I did my best to focus. My grades slid, though. I couldn't bring myself to pay attention in class. My only instinct was to rest my head on the desk and concentrate on not crying. My math teacher called Papi.

"What's happening with Diane?" he asked. "She doesn't seem as interested in her work anymore."

"I'll talk to her," Papi promised. "I'm sure she'll get back on track soon." Of course, he didn't dare tell the guy the reality—that our family was being pulled apart by forces we had no control over. That I was practically motherless for the time being. That my brother was living away from home. That we were trapped in a living nightmare.

Seventh grade is when things began changing for me physically. Ah, puberty—you wonderful, natural, normal, yet . . . awkward friend. I was developing boobs; not gigantic ones, mind you—but they were big enough for me to need some kind of a bra. Mami had always been the one to be sure I had the clothes and undergarments I needed. She'd buy me cute cotton undies and girly dresses. Now, what choice did I have but to ask my dad?

"Papi?" I said, one night after he got home from work. "Um, I need a bra."

"What?" he said.

"I think it's time for me to get a bra," I repeated, cringing. My face was the color of strawberry jam.

"Honey," he told me, "I don't think so. You're good."

But I insisted. It was the most embarrassing thing in the world to be talking to my dad about a bra, but a girl has to do what a girl has to do. For a whole week, I begged him. Finally, he agreed.

He drove to a store in a strip mall. I clutched the seat belt on the way over, consoling myself with the thought that this errand probably wouldn't take *that* long and that soon it'd be over. We parked and headed straight to the preteen undies section. I wanted to get this over with as quickly as possible— so I grabbed the first bra I saw.

"That's too big for you," my father told me. "It's not going to fit." I wasn't positive, but I thought he might just be hiding a smile. I was clearly clueless about what to pick.

I slid it back on the rack and picked up another. It was pink and cotton and lace-trimmed. "That might work," he said. I grabbed three of them in various colors and practically ran straight to the checkout. Like, let's get out of here, already!

Later on, Papi called Mami and told her about our adventure; both thought it was hilarious. "I'm so sorry I'm not there to help with this," she said to me, half laughing, half incredibly sad that she was missing out.

"It's no big deal," I told her, trying to be brisk. "Whatever. It's just a bra." But truthfully, I wished so hard she'd been there. Showing my pain wasn't going to bring her back, though. Seeming unfazed on the outside allowed me to hide how vulnerable I felt on the inside.

I finally had my bra. Now I just needed to get my period. It seemed every girl at school except for me had gotten hers. Mami had already told me all about what to expect. "Has it come yet?" she kept asking me from Colombia. "If it comes, tell your dad right away. And call me. You can also talk to Olivia."

Every morning, I'd examine my underwear for any sign of red. Nothing. After a couple of months of paying close attention, I was so over it. I was like, *This is never going to happen.*

Until one evening, it did. Papi was in the living room,

glued to a soccer match, when I emerged from the bathroom with a weird look on my face.

"What's wrong?" he asked.

"Um, I'm bleeding," I told him. I began to cry.

He turned off the TV and stood. "It's okay, Diane," he said, pulling me into his arms. "It's natural. Don't cry there, *chibola*. I'm here for you." Never had I missed my mother more than I did in that moment.

There's only one thing more cringeworthy than buying a bra with your father—and that is buying maxi pads with him. Dad was cool about it, though, and tried to make me feel comfortable. We left there with every kind known to womankind: Regular absorbency pads. Heavy flow pads. Panty liners. It was all good. Until, of course, I started flushing them down the toilet. No one had told me that I should throw them out! Furthermore, if I saw even the tiniest trace of blood, I was through with that pad. Papi, who came into the restroom after I'd just used it, took notice.

"Diane, can I talk to you for a sec, dear?" he said. *Uh-oh.* I nodded.

"You need to wrap your pads and put them in the wastebasket," he informed me. "Oh, and one more thing: You should wait at least a couple of hours before you grab a new one." Both of us blushed. But I got the point, and I was grateful for his advice.

By Christmas of my eighth-grade year, I'd fully accepted

that Mami wasn't going to return. My mind went straight to blaming myself. I must've done something so unforgivable that no round of Hail Marys had been sufficient to keep her with us. This must be God's will. Papi seemed to have accepted that as well. With time, we each adjusted to the reality that life would have to move forward with or without her in it.

And then . . . she came back. For the second time. In January 2000. Not to Boston this time, but to New Jersey. The circumstances of her getting here were as mysterious to me as the last time. I knew better than to press either of my parents about it. She moved in with her sister's son, my cousin whom I loved very much.

The first time we went to visit her in New Jersey, it wasn't exactly a sweet reunion. She was obviously thrilled to be back—"I can't believe I'm here with you again!" she kept saying as she hugged me—but honestly, I had mixed feelings. Of course I'd missed her. I'd yearned to have her close again. But I was scared that she'd get arrested again. Scared of yet another disappointment, that she'd be shackled and taken away from us. I didn't think my heart could take it.

During our visits to New Jersey, Papi and Mami tried not to argue in front of me. But that didn't last long; I heard all the dirt. Papi was still furious about how careless Mami had been in requesting that paperwork. And then again when she had walked the kids to school. And while he knew how deeply she'd missed us, he worried about how dangerous her journey back into America was.

In February of my eighth-grade year, Papi and I moved from that basement into a two-family house in Roxbury. The neighborhood was frickin' scary. Gunshots rang out at midnight. Reports of stabbings made the headlines. Graffiti covered the buildings, and music blasted from car stereos. It wasn't far, but at least we wouldn't be at the same address if ICE turned up. Mami moved in with us shortly after that, and from there, things started to look up.

There were some bumps in the beginning of our reunion. Truth is, though, even amid their bickering and the chaos, Mami and Papi's love for each other was still strong. And within days of her return, his spirits lifted. They argued, but with Eric out of the house, there was a lot less to fight about. Papi was still hopeful about that lawyer; he'd assured us that, even with Mami's troubles, he could continue moving forward on Papi's case. And for the first time, I had my own room. Because we were in a different house—and, I hoped, out of reach of ICE—I felt safe enough to actually sleep at night. Maybe I'd done something right to please the father above.

Overall, it didn't take long for things to feel back to normal—whatever normal is in a story like mine.

Right to left: Gabriela, me, and Dana at our eighth-grade graduation

7

THE PLAN

Y ou all right, sweetie?" My guidance counselor was peering at me, concerned.

I slumped over in the seat across from her desk, my face in my palms. Near the end of the school day, I'd come by for our scheduled appointment. What was supposed to be a quick check-in had turned into a cryfest.

It was May 2000. In two short months, I'd be done with eighth grade—which meant it was time for me to choose a high school. And if you think my middle school sounded rough, it was nothing compared with the neighborhood high schools. So I began strategizing my way into a better school. I had lifted my grades from so-so to admirable, but despite all that work, my GPA wasn't soaring. I applied to private and charter schools, thinking I'd qualify for financial aid, but

I was rejected from all of them. I was fresh out of options—and no amount of comforting and tissues could change that.

"You know what, Diane?" the counselor said, her face brightening. "I don't know why I didn't think of this earlier, but I know something else we could try."

I stopped sniveling and sat up. "What?" I asked curiously.

"There's this performing arts school that opened a few years back," she said. She sifted through a stack of brochures on her desk and pulled out a leaflet. "Here it is," she said, smiling. "It's the Boston Arts Academy."

The pamphlet's front cover pictured a boy playing the violin and another one painting; in a third photo, a girl was in a dance pose. I leafed through it a page at a time. "Has the application deadline passed?" I asked. This looked too good to be true; there had to be a catch.

"I don't think so," she said, and googled the school's name. A few clicks later, she said, "You're in luck. It says here that the audition deadline is still three weeks away."

I raised my eyebrows. "You mean I have to *audition*?"

"That's right," she said, chuckling. "You'll have to try out. But you love to sing. You'd be great for this."

With the pamphlet in my backpack, I headed out to the library. There, on a public computer, I read up on Boston Arts Academy. It turned out that it was the city's only public high school for the visual and performing arts. My heart did a little happy dance at the thought of being one of those smiling, artistic students.

"How was your day?" Mami asked when I shuffled through the door later. "Fine," I responded, careful not to mention BAA. I didn't want to jinx my chances.

That evening, long after Mami and Papi said good night, I pulled out a blue journal I kept hidden under my pillow. I turned to a page and wrote two large words across the top: *My Audition*. Beneath the heading, I scribbled every song I'd imagined performing. *I could do some Mariah Carey*, I thought with a divalike hair flip. *Or maybe a Broadway show tune*. I chewed the top of my pen. Just thinking about this was *fun*. The list stretched on for pages until, my eyelids heavy with exhaustion, I drifted off into dreams.

Back to Eric. He had been doing well in New Jersey. With the encouragement of my uncle, he'd nailed down a few handyman gigs and began studying for the GED to get his high school diploma. Then—trouble erupted. One morning when he was on his way to work, metal toolbox in hand, three dudes pulled up to him and started beating him up. Desperately, Eric flung his toolbox at them in self-defense. Next thing he knew, the police arrived and they arrested all four. Although the three other guys had been the wrong-doers, they pressed assault charges against Eric. A court date was set.

On the scheduled day, none of the attackers showed up to court. Eric couldn't afford an attorney, so the court appointed one for him. This attorney suggested what he thought was the best legal strategy. "Just sign this paper and say you were stalking them," he told Eric. "Stalking is a misdemeanor—and you'll be able to walk free." My brother felt conflicted. Why should he confess to something he never *did*? But, thinking the lawyer knew better than he did, he took the advice. And boy, was it bad advice. Besides admitting to a crime he hadn't committed, what he didn't know was that Gloria, who was considering divorce, had put a hold on his citizenship application. That meant Eric's "misdemeanor" was grounds for his automatic deportation.

Days later, things got real—fast. Eric was shackled, put into a detention center, and shipped back to Colombia. It all happened so quickly that Mami, Papi, and I didn't see him before his departure.

Mami was crushed. Her only son, her firstborn—the child she'd brought to America with a hope shared by millions of parents—had not just lost his footing, he had also been cheated out of a chance to make it in America.

"I wish we could've done more," she said to Papi through tears on the day Eric was deported. "I hate the way things turned out."

"We did what we could," Papi comforted her. "It was out of our hands."

Eric had been disenchanted with his life here for a while. Besides not having citizenship, he felt like the odd child out in our family. Even once he turned himself around in New Jersey, hard luck knocked him to his knees. He'd gotten caught up with a rowdy crowd. And as an undocumented brown boy, his mistakes brought on more than just detention or a slap on the wrist—they cost him his opportunity for citizenship.

I last saw my brother in this country in 2000—the spring of my eighth-grade year. My heart broke that day. I missed him terribly. I longed for our trips to the pizzeria. Our Sunday TV marathons, cackling in unison at cartoons. Those times when he'd pick me up and swing me around until I pleaded, through giggles, for him to put me down. And yet, as much as I wished to be with him, an unspoken truth hung in the air. Now Mami and Papi had one less child to provide for— and that meant a stronger chance at their most fervent prayer.

Papi never missed a payment to the immigration lawyer. For months, he handed over the money he'd scrambled together with weekend janitorial and factory work. His working conditions at the factory were horrible and unsafe. His boss humiliated and threatened him, and paid him late, if at all. The disturbing truth is that his boss knew he could get away with being cruel to workers—they were too afraid to fight back, for fear of being arrested and deported.

Papi worked so often that I saw him less and less. Mami took on extra babysitting and housecleaning. Hopeful for a fresh start, they also ramped up their skills: Papi tried another English class at the community college; my mother enrolled in a computer course.

Every couple of weeks, my father called to check on the case. "How's it looking?" he'd ask the attorney. "Are we getting close?"

"I can't say for sure," the guy often told him, "but it shouldn't be much longer, probably a few more months. We're making good progress."

One week, Papi left two messages for the guy. Usually he'd get a call back within a day. This time, his calls went unreturned. Papi furrowed his brow with concern. "He's probably out of town," Mami consoled him. "I'm sure everything's fine." The next week, Papi called again. Silence. That's when my father chose a different approach. "Come on, Diane," he said to me one afternoon, coat in hand. "Let's go see him."

Through the sliding doors of the office building and up the elevator, Papi didn't say much. I could tell he was nervous. The walk down that corridor, which had always been long, now seemed to stretch into eternity. When we reached the office door, something wasn't right. The lawyer's nameplate was missing. Papi and I glanced at each other, not sure what it meant. My dad placed his palm on the door's handle. It was unlocked.

The room was dark. Papi flipped on the fluorescent lights to reveal an empty space. No desk. No Harvard diploma. No forms for clients to fill out. Just a stack of cardboard boxes and some rolls of packing tape. Except for the nail upon which the Lady Justice picture had hung, the walls were bare. I turned to Papi, whose brown eyes widened. He put his hand on his head. "*No me lo puedo creer*," he murmured almost inaudibly. "I can't believe it."

He rushed back to the door and dashed into the hall; I followed him, my breath heavy. We rang the bell to the next office down the hall, a dental practice. A secretary, this elderly Irish woman in reading glasses and with a poodle-curl perm, let us in. She looked up from her clipboard.

"May I help you, sir?" she said.

Papi stared over at me—which was my cue to speak up. "Um," I said, "do you know that lawyer at the end of the hall?"

"Yes," she answered. "What about him?"

"Well," I said, "his office is cleared out. We're wondering where he is."

She squinted at me over the top edge of her reading glasses. "Oh, I don't know," she said. "I think I saw some moving guys here last week." She returned her attention to her clipboard.

We walked back to the office as if, magically, the attorney might've reappeared. My father paced across the floor and slowly looked from one corner to the next. "How could this happen?" he repeated, his voice quivering more each time he said the words. "I don't understand. *Ayúdame, Dios.*" His eyes filled with tears.

Later, at home, in a moment I'd wish upon no child, I saw my papi, my rock, crumble before my eyes. "Why?" he said over and over, rubbing his head in disbelief. He simply could not believe he'd been taken advantage of in this way. What kind of hope could he offer his family? Himself, even? Witnessing my father in that state broke my heart. I whispered, "It's okay, Papi. I'm sure we can figure this out."

Even as I spoke those words, I knew they weren't true. What was there to figure out? My parents had forked over thousands of dollars. Nearly everything they had was given to that crook. For almost two years, Papi had worked nonstop to improve our family's position, believing that he could give us a better existence. Instead, what he found was an abandoned office. A fake lawyer who'd strung him along with broken promises. And little money left to his name.

That "lawyer" had picked on the most vulnerable people. Just like Papi's factory boss, he knew that we, and other people in our position, couldn't go to the police to report him without risking getting arrested ourselves. Robin Hood stole from the rich to give to the poor. Well, this sucker stole from the poor to make himself rich.

I lowered myself onto the carpet and scooted right next to Papi. I put my arms around his neck, and, with tears streaming down my cheeks, I embraced him for the longest time. I cried not just because my dad's latest effort at citizenship had fallen apart. Mostly I cried because someone I cared for so much, someone I'd watched fight with everything in him, was hurting beyond words.

Papi tried an old number he had for the lady who'd put us in touch with the attorney. She didn't answer. Later, neighbors told us that this woman was actually *working* for this fake lawyer; for each unsuspecting and vulnerable undocumented worker she'd bring him, he gave her five hundred dollars. And the Harvard degree? Yet another lie.

Dinner that evening was the quietest in the history of our house. Mami sat stone-faced and sullen. "Maybe he's coming back," she said. "You should go over there again tomorrow." She couldn't accept that we'd been scammed. Dad didn't respond. He got up from the table and left his meal half-eaten. I stared down at my food and said nothing.

Sabrina and me on July 21, 2000, in Dedham, Massachusetts. My first grown-up birthday dinner at Uno's with the girls. *Picture credit: Gabriela V.*

8

GROUND SHIFT

My audition for Boston Arts Academy was the following week. Shyly, I finally told Mami about my plans to apply. "Wow, that's wonderful!" she said. She was excited for me, of course, but we were both heavy-hearted from the recent blow. In a way, that setback made me more certain that I needed to build a life for myself, one not dependent on my parents. For me, this was more than a tryout. It was my way out of the hood.

On the morning of the audition, I rose early, showered, and put on my favorite sundress. Mami insisted I have breakfast. She made me oatmeal before I headed off for the T train that would take me to the Fenway area of Boston. I must've looked like a tourist because my eyes darted every which way with wonder as I stumbled through the doors of the music department. A perky blond assistant greeted me.

"You must be Diane! Come on in," she said, leading me up a flight of stairs and into a back room. There, a group of about ten other kids had assembled. A Dominican-looking girl was warming up with some scales. A dude with short dreads and glasses had his eyes glued to sheet music. Neither of them looked over at me. They *seemed* confident, but who knew? Maybe they were just as nervous as I was.

"Wait here until we call for you. And good luck," the assistant said.

When my name was called, I smoothed my dress and strode into the music room, a mix of confidence and a shamble of nerves. A voice in my head echoed "Relax! Breathe!"

"What are you singing for us today?" asked Mr. Stewart, the head of the music department.

"I'll be singing 'Si tú eres mi hombre,' which is the Spanish version of 'Power of Love' by Céline Dion." I'd also do "L-O-V-E," an American standard made popular by Frank Sinatra.

"Let's hear it," said Mr. Stewart. My heart was racing, but heck, it was now or never.

When I finished, I looked to his face for approval. "Thank you, Diane," he said, staying poker-faced. "We'll be in touch."

"That's it?!" I blurted out.

He laughed. "Yes, that's it." My heart just about fell into

my shoes. Every day after that audition took place, my eye was glued to the mailbox. I wanted to be ready to pounce whenever BAA sent me their verdict. *Would I be accepted? Would this be another rejection? Would I be stuck going to that scary school?* Two weeks later, I had my answer. I scurried out to our yard the second I spotted the mailwoman pulling up to our mailbox. "Anything for me today?" I asked innocently. She rummaged through a handful of envelopes and stopped when she reached a large manila one. "I bet this is what you've been waiting on, young lady," she said, handing it over.

My name, in all capital letters, was on the front. Breathless, I pried it open, at first gently, and then with full force. A stack of paper slid out; on top lay a typed letter on fancy ivory-colored paper. I flipped it over and I scanned the first paragraph urgently. My eyes fell on two sentences: "We are pleased to offer you enrollment for the fall of 2000," it read. "Congratulations, and welcome to Boston Arts Academy!" Was I being played? I stared down at the words, rereading them to be sure my eyes hadn't deceived me. My hands trembled along the edges of the letter. And during a moment that will forever live in my memory, the world, for once, was perfect. I, the kid who's shy on the outside and bursting with song on the inside, had been accepted.

It's funny how somewhere you've never been before can already feel like home. Attending Boston Arts Academy was just that. For the first time, I fit in. No one teased me for striving to participate and study hard. I could be myself and let my geek flag fly. I still had to be chill around the neighborhood—I'm cool, dog—but in school my guard lowered. I'd found my people—artists who, like me, wanted to learn and explore. The only downside was that my crew—Dana, Gabriela, and Sabrina—wasn't in class with me; Dana had moved to Florida, and Sabrina was at West Roxbury and liked it. And Gabriela was at our worst nightmare, English High School in Jamaica Plain.

Believe it or not, showing up for school was actually fun. Every day brought something exciting. In the cafeteria during lunch, students gave theater or musical performances. Artists like filmmaker Spike Lee and cellist Yo-Yo Ma visited campus and gave us talks about craft, creativity, and staying motivated. We took field trips to the Boston Symphony, the Museum of Fine Arts, and the ballet.

I was blown away by the opportunity laid out before me. I was motivated to give 100 percent and keep my grades on point. Teachers talked about college as if they assumed we'd each enroll. What a difference exposure to these people and places made for me. I often thought to myself: *If only I'd realized sooner that I had just as much right to access art and culture as anyone else did!* Simply being in this new environment lifted my expectations for what was possible in my life, even with the uncertainty at home. And the more art and music and theater I saw, the more I knew that I didn't just want to be an admiring audience member—I wanted to be a participant.

BAA's curriculum was designed to be like college courses and discussions. This was perfect for the inner-city kid who often felt left out of the political conversation. Students were always pushed to think outside the box and to think deeply about challenging issues. Discussions about race, ethnicity, and different cultures were encouraged. Social class— meaning poverty, wealth, and everything in between—was an issue that affected all our lives, and discussing it felt grown-up and interesting. Being asked to think about these things felt like a demonstration of the teachers' respect for us. It showed us that they thought we were smart enough to handle it.

The more I read and talked with my friends, the more I thought about my status in a culture that values some lives— whether they are wealthier or whiter, or of a certain religion or gender—over others. I'd always been bewildered by the privileges our white counterparts in Newton and Wellesley had over us. But I was starting to realize that their DNA or zip code wasn't better than mine—they were just born into different lives.

Oh, so I wasn't *born a loser*, I thought, relieved. There are systems that exist in the country that are to other people's advantages, not mine. Good to know. There is a belief that destiny is in our hands, and it is to a degree. But there are also circumstances and fortunes (or misfortunes) that we were all born into.

Music class was my favorite. About forty of us divided up into our sections: soprano (me), alto, tenor, and bass. There is something special when a group of people reach for a common goal—that's what singing in harmony is. A gospel song like "Joyful, Joyful," "Edelweiss" from *The Sound of Music*, hits from *Jesus Christ Superstar* and *Rent*—in my head, I can still hear them. We would prepare for different events during the year. The two big ones were winter fest and spring fest.

At the end of chorus one day that March, Mr. Stewart pulled my classmate Damien and me aside. "May I see you two for a sec?" he asked.

"Um . . . okay," I stammered. My mind raced. *Am I in trouble?*

"As you know," he said, "spring fest is coming. Well, I'd like to offer you both a special part. It'd be amazing if you'd sing a duet."

Damien and I looked at each other. This was like being asked to be on the varsity team without even playing JV. "Are you sure? Me? Really?" I said, letting out a nervous giggle.

"Do you want it or do you not?" he said, chuckling.

"Yeah, sure," I piped up. Damien also agreed, grinning. The following week, we started staying after school to learn our number. It was a soaring love song duet from the musical *Miss Saigon* called "The Last Night of the World."

Despite the upswing my life at school had taken, things at home remained unstable. Mami and Papi were nowhere close to citizenship, and they knew it. At night behind closed doors, I'd hear them arguing about what to do next. Understandably, they were suspicious of reaching out for legal help. They kept up their daily work grind to gradually rebuild their savings. They couldn't afford to sign up for other English or computer classes, and besides, they scarcely had time anyway in between working.

I stopped even asking for updates. Secretly, I'd started to give up on the dream that they'd reach their goal. All I had was the hope that they'd remain under the radar until I was old enough to help.

We'd been seeing less and less of little Erica. That changed in early 2001. Gloria made it clear that, even with Eric gone, she wanted us to be part of the little girl's life. In the evenings, I'd spread toys across my bed so we could play together. "Hi, sweetie," I'd say, flashing a Disney coloring book in her direction. With a smile, she'd pick up a crayon, only to wander off a second later and bang on her mini xylophone. With that cutie in the house, there was never a dull moment.

One afternoon that May, I was entertaining Erica in the

living room. Mami was in the kitchen with her friend. I over-heard their conversation.

"I had the strangest dream last night," Mami said. She lifted the lid on a pot, poked her spoon inside, and scooped out some soup to taste. "I can't remember the whole thing, but at the end of it, I fell into a pond of dead fish."

"A pond of dead fish? Hmm . . ." Mami's friend was known to be clairvoyant and often could feel things . . . supernatural things. Her talent, whether it was real or not, sort of gave me the creeps. I already worried our family had bad juju. Our unknown fate was frightening enough without some shady predictions.

"I woke up in a cold sweat," my mom said in a serious tone. "I have a bad feeling about it. Maybe some bad luck is coming."

Right then, Papi walked in. "Are you telling *that* story again, Maria?" he said, chuckling. Apparently, he'd already heard it that morning. "You're going to scare Diane. You're being superstitious. I'm sure it's no big deal." Mami smirked, began slicing some onions, and changed the topic.

On Papi's way home from the factory later that week, he stopped at a bodega to pick up a couple of items. The cashier offered him a Powerball ticket. At first Papi declined, but then he said, "Okay, might as well give it a shot." He paid the man, tucked the ticket in his pocket, and forgot about it. Following dinner, he kicked off his shoes and turned on the news. When an announcer mentioned the live lotto drawing, Papi remembered his ticket.

"Maria! *¡Chibola!*" he shouted, charging into the living room a moment later. "Guess what?" Mami and I had been watching the telenovela *Yo soy Betty, la fea*, the Colombian version; the first and best version. (Back up, all you new versions of *Ugly Betty!*) We bolted to our feet.

"What is it?" Mami said.

"My numbers match!" screamed my father, waving the ticket. "We won ten thousand dollars!"

"Are you sure, honey?" Mami said, taking the ticket from my father in disbelief.

Papi raced back out of the room and returned with a piece of paper; on it, he'd scribbled the row of digits. "Look," he exclaimed, handing my mother the evidence.

Mami's eyes darted back and forth between the paper and the ticket. We all got quiet while she examined the numbers. The silence was deafening. "Oh my God, you're right!" she finally cried out, giving my father a huge kiss. "I guess my dream didn't mean anything!" she hollered. "We're lucky after all!"

For some families, maybe the well-heeled ones in Wellesley, Massachusetts, ten thousand dollars wouldn't even cover the cost of spring break. For us, it was like a million bucks. And literally overnight, my parents went from feeling hopeless to optimistic. "We can use this money to pay a legitimate lawyer," Papi told Mami the next morning. "This is a miracle."

When Papi claimed his lotto money, he came home wearing the biggest grin. After so many months of turmoil, seeing his magical smile again made me feel fuzzy inside. I couldn't stop grinning, either. Maybe I'd been wrong to doubt that things would ever work out. Finally!

On his way out the door that Thursday, Papi poked his head into my room. I blinked my eyes awake.

"Good morning, honey," he said.

"Hi, Papi," I answered with a yawn. "Everything okay?"

He nodded and stepped in. "I want you to have this," he told me—and that's when he handed me that brand-new fifty-dollar bill. My eyes popped open. I slid from my bed and hugged him. "Thanks, Papi," I said, floored. "I love you." Every morning I'd wake up to three dollars on the nightstand, but this was generous in a way that surpassed my expectations. Papi beamed proudly at me and hugged me tight.

It was still pretty early when my father left in the morning, so I decided to squeeze in one more hour of rest. An hour and a half later, my eyelids flew open. I'd overslept. *Shoot*—I'd be running late for school.

For more than a decade, I've relived every detail of what happened during the next twelve hours. Arguing with Mami. Rushing to school. The eerie feeling in my gut. Rehearsal with Damien, sneaker shopping, and the voice on our machine saying no one was home, playing on a loop in my head. On the evening of May 17, 2001, out of breath and full of dread, I flung open our front door. Nothing has been the same since.

Me and Papi, Mama and Eric.

2017 family selfie

9

TAKEN

A dark entryway was all there was to greet me. The house was as silent as an empty church. No noise from the television. No chattering in Spanish. No salsa blasting from the radio. I noticed the light on in the kitchen. I darted toward it, my heart pounding with each pace.

"Mami!" I called out. "Papi! Are you here?"

A plate of sliced plantains rested on the kitchen counter; a pot of uncooked rice was on the stove's back burner. The faucet, which Papi had been trying to fix that week, leaked into the sink. *Drip. Drip. Drip.* On the table, that morning's newspaper lay next to a half-filled cup of coffee. Mami's apron, which she always folded and put away after preparing a meal, was dangling from a chair back. I pivoted to the hall and dashed to my parents' room. *Could they be sleeping?*

"Where is everyone?" I screamed at the top of my lungs. "Mami, Papi—I'm home!" I pushed on their bedroom door. It was stuck. "Are you guys here?" I yelled, banging on the wood with my fists. "Open up!" I wedged the toe of my new Adidas into the lower right corner of the door to force it open. Mami's address book was open atop her nightstand; Papi's reading glasses lay near the foot of their bed. With my entire body shaking, I rushed to the bathroom. Then into my room. Then back to the kitchen. And finally, with a prayer that they might be outdoors, into the backyard.

Empty.

Right then, the doorbell shrieked. The sound in the silent household sent a shock up my spine. I stopped. *Could it be them?* At the door, I stood on tiptoes to look into the peephole. There stood the neighbor who lived on the other side of our two-family house, a squat middle-aged woman who hadn't ever been very friendly to us. I furrowed my brow.

"It's me, Diane," she said. "Unlock the door."

This was unexpected. She'd never voluntarily come to talk to us. My hands quivered as I slid the chain left and unlatched it. With my face flushed and my stomach churning, I stepped into the vestibule.

"Your parents have been taken," she said plainly, as if she was reporting the weather forecast.

"Um, what?" I blustered. My head felt like it was about to

fall off my shoulders, tumble to the ground, and burst open right there in front of her. "What do you mean?"

"I mean the immigration officers came here and arrested them," she shot back. "They're gone."

I glared at her, suddenly dizzy. The foyer was spinning, faster and faster, like I was stuck in a washing machine. "No!" I wailed with my palms over my temples. I swayed forward, then back, and caught myself before falling onto the linoleum. "They're not gone!" I squealed. The woman didn't blink.

"Anyone you want me to call?" she asked, practically backing away from me. I was too distraught to answer. My moans turned to howls.

"Well," she said, realizing I wasn't going to respond, "let me know if you need anything, okay?" I didn't answer. I staggered into the house and slammed the door.

What am I going to do? My thoughts raced faster than my heartbeat. *I need to call someone.* I hurried to the living room and called my niece's mother, Gloria. *Ring. Ring. Ring.* She picked up.

"Hello, Gloria?" I whimpered.

She paused. "What's wrong, Diane?"

"My parents have been taken!" I cried into the receiver. Hot tears splashed onto my T-shirt.

"What are you talking about?" she asked.

"The police came here and arrested them!" I hollered back.

Dead silence.

Even in my panic, I was already trying to find a way to fix things—to make sure I was safe. "Can I stay with you?" I asked between gasps. "Maybe you can move in here. I can watch Erica for you. I'll go to school and get a job."

"Diane, that's not a good idea," Gloria said. She explained that her mother believed that further involvement with my family and me might somehow lead to Erica being deported to Colombia, too. This caught me off guard. After all, Erica, like me, was born a citizen of the United States. She *couldn't* be deported. It seemed like Gloria had already made up her mind, though, so I didn't protest. Instead, I sniveled, "So what am I supposed to do?"

"For now," she said, "don't open your door for anyone. We don't really know what's happening yet. The police might return there. Stay out of sight until we can figure something out."

I scurried back to the front door to double-check that it was chained and bolted. I turned off every light, closed all the blinds, went into my room, and locked the door. Phone in hand, I got on the floor and scooted all the way under the bed. Our house had never felt so quiet or scary.

I cried as softly as I could, my dad's words reverberating in my head. "If anything ever happens to us," he'd often told me, "you've gotta be strong." Strong? I felt like the wind had been kicked out of me. I felt weak and here I was, alone and abandoned. I called another lifeline—Amelia, the mother of my friend Gabriela.

"Amelia?" I whispered.

She picked up on my distress. "What's going on, sweetie?" she asked. After I explained, she said, "Where are you?"

"Under my bed."

"Stay where you are," she told me. "Don't move. I'll be there as soon as I can."

Minutes later, she was at the front door. I looked through the peephole to confirm it was her and not the police. After opening the door, I fell right into her arms. "It's okay, Diane," she repeated as she stroked my hair. "Everything's going to be fine now."

The phone rang again. Papi.

"Hector?" Amelia said, her voice firm. "Yes, I'm here with Diane." I listened intently to Amelia's side of the conversation and pieced together how the day had unfolded. My parents had been taken separately. Mami, who'd been making dinner, was arrested in the late afternoon while Papi was on his way home from work. My father pulled into the driveway to discover that the immigration officers had surrounded the house; they were waiting to put him in handcuffs. Papi was driven to a facility for men, Mami to one for women. My father was allowed to make one short call. This was it.

Amelia, shaking her head in sorrow at what she'd heard, handed the phone to me. "Your father wants to speak to you," she said.

"Papi"—my voice was scratchy from screaming earlier— "where are you?"

"Listen to me, Diane," he said sternly. "Don't be afraid. You're a smart girl." My eyes filled with a fresh round of tears. "Don't cry, Diane. Do not cry. Now I need you to pay attention," he continued, "because I don't have much longer on the phone. Go in our room and pack our suitcases, one for me and one for your mother. We'll need our things in Colombia."

"What?" I shrieked. Mami and Papi had been in prison for less than twenty-four hours, yet my father was convinced they'd be deported. "But can't we do something to stop this?"

"There's nothing we can do," he said matter-of-factly. The only way he and Mami might have a chance at staying, he explained, was if a top-level attorney took their case; even with Papi's lotto luck, he didn't have the money for a pricey lawyer. "I've asked Amelia if you can stay with her," he told me. In the background of the phone I could hear a guard ordering Papi to finish his call. "So you'll be with her, okay? I love you. I've gotta go now." *Click.* I put down the phone.

Packing my own parents' bags for their journey back to Colombia—was there a crueler punishment? *Pull yourself together, Diane*, I told myself, bracing for the task.

I had no clue where to begin. What do you pack for the two people you love most in the world? For two people who may never return? I searched through their drawers and closet, pulling out random items. Shirts, pants, shoes. A couple of coats and sweaters. Was it enough? Nothing else would fit, so it'd have to be. *Done.*

As I zipped the luggage, I heard noises. I peeked out the door and into the hall. The commotion was coming from the kitchen. I made my way there. When I reached the doorway, neighbors from our street peered at me. Word about my parents' capture had apparently spread. Amelia had let them in, thinking they'd come by to offer me their sympathies.

That is not at all what they were there to do, though.

One of the women was standing in front of our open fridge with a large plastic bag in her hand. She was packing up our fruits and vegetables.

"What are you doing?" I asked.

She looked up. "Your parents won't need this food anymore," she snapped. "We might as well take it."

"Excuse me." Amelia stepped in, suddenly realizing what was going on. "Can you please put that back and leave?" The lady glared at her and slammed the fridge closed without returning the food she'd taken.

I was dumbfounded. I was already feeling so vulnerable, and the people my parents had called friends were stealing from our home. It was the ultimate insult. And ironically, it was in that moment, one with others surrounding me, that I felt most alone and uncared for. I marched from the kitchen and locked every door in the house.

Now that I was moving in with Gaby, I needed to prepare a bag for myself. I packed school clothes, books, and a Norma Jean mini Cabbage Patch doll that Papi had given me for Christmas. When I went into the bathroom to gather my toiletries, more tears flowed. All around me were signs of what my parents thought would be an ordinary evening. Mami's rosary hanging on the towel rack. Papi's cotton balls that he'd stuff into his ears before he showered. I opened the medicine cabinet, took out my toothbrush, and shut the glass again. There, in the mirror, I gazed at a face I didn't know. My own. It looked hollow and tired. Puffy eyes stared back at me. My numb lips were bitten and raw.

Amelia tapped on the bathroom door. "You all right, hon?" she asked.

"I'll be out in a sec," I told her.

Once we'd dragged the suitcases to her Camry, we did a final walk-through of the house to secure it. In the living room, I looked to be sure I wasn't leaving behind anything private or urgent. I knew I wasn't coming back here.

Amelia's home in Roslindale was only ten minutes from us. She shared a small house with her son and two daughters; Gabriela was the youngest. When we pulled into the driveway, my best friend was waiting outside for me. "I'm so glad you're here," she said, embracing me. Because I'd spent so much time at Gabriela's, it thankfully felt familiar. Comfortable. Safe. Amelia also did all she could to welcome me. "Here you are," she said, giving me fresh linens and towels. "Make yourself at home."

Only hours had passed since my parents had been detained, yet I'd already resolved something in my heart. I would not leave Boston. I would not throw away the miracle I'd been given to attend Boston Arts Academy. Getting into that school was the greatest thing that had happened to me— and I was not willing to give it up by moving to my aunt and uncle's in New Jersey, or to my parents' place in Colombia, or anywhere that wasn't a bus or subway ride away from school.

That evening in the dark, squeezing my Norma Jean doll, I stared up at the ceiling and thought of how the week had begun. Mami's bizarre dream. Papi's stroke of luck and the joy on his face upon winning the money. I thought of the thousands of moments, large and small, that had led me to this house. This bed. This life. I tried not to cry, because I didn't want to wake Gabriela. But I couldn't help it. She heard me sniffling and sat up.

"You scared?" she asked me, her voice kind.

"Yes," I answered.

"I know," she said. "What you're going through is scary."

A wave of comfort washed over me. Finally, someone was validating what I was feeling. Being strong is necessary; it helps you move forward and keeps you brave. But honoring your true feelings is necessary, too, and mine were sadness, fear, and loneliness. In this moment, my friend hadn't urged me to be strong. She hadn't told me that everything would be just fine. Rather, she'd given me permission, right before sleep, to be the frightened little girl that I was.

Me and Papi, Mama and Vanilla Ice—(cough) I mean, my big bro, Eric

10
A NEW REALITY

The morning after the nightmare, I opened my eyes and looked around slowly. *Where am I?* And then all at once, the horrible memory of the day before came flooding back. *Yes*, I thought. *It really happened.*

I went to school that day. Amelia dropped me off on her way to her nurse's assistant job. My body was there, sleepwalking through the halls, but my head was in the sky. At least school was a distraction. And with spring fest on the way, I couldn't bear to miss rehearsal for the one good thing I had going for me.

Pain and humiliation mingled in my heart. As usual, I kept my home life under wraps. That afternoon during chorus, Mr. Stewart sensed something was off with me. "You okay?" he asked, concerned. I nodded and mustered a fake smile. He looked like he knew I was hiding something, but he didn't pry.

Over the next week, Mami and Papi called from prison. The conversations were all the same—tears, apologies, instructions on what to do. As Papi suspected, their chances of remaining here were minuscule.

"Has anyone from Immigration tried to contact you?" my father asked.

"No," I told him. Neither ICE nor the Massachusetts's Department of Children and Families had contacted me. This meant that at fourteen, I'd been left on my own. Literally. The same authorities who deported my parents hadn't bothered to check whether I, a fourteen-year-old citizen of this country, would be left without a family, adult supervision, or even a home.

On the other hand, if the authorities *did* find me, then there was the nightmarish possibility of being put into foster care with complete strangers. Anytime the thought of it came up, I pushed it out of my brain with dread. To be put in a "family" I hadn't chosen meant I'd really be out of control of my life, my future. What kind of household would I be put into? Who were social workers and cops to know which family was right for me? Would they even care about matching me up with the right people?

I'm fortunate that Amelia agreed to take me in temporarily, but no one in our government was aware that she'd done so. In the eyes of ICE, it was as if I didn't exist. I'd been completely invisible to them.

My future was unsure—but as long as I stayed with Amelia, I knew I was loved and cared for.

Two weeks after my parents were sent to prison, Amelia took me to visit Papi. By then, both he and Mami had been transferred from jails in Boston to detention centers in New Hampshire. One part of me longed to see my father, but another part dreaded the visit. Seeing my dignified, loving dad in prison would be painful. People in prison are thought of as criminals, thugs, gangsters. No matter who they might be, what they've done or haven't done—they're also, like my parents, humans. People with families. He deserved all the respect in the world, and I cringed at the thought of him in chains.

Barbed-wire fence surrounded the brown-brick buildings. The security checkpoints were guarded by guards and barking Dobermans. I couldn't believe that a man who'd never jaywalked or run a red light had been sent to a place like this.

Inside, our purses were searched like at an airport. Once we'd made it through the metal detector, we dropped off the suitcase I'd packed for Papi.

We were led to a large, windowless area where about fifty others were waiting. A few people were alone. Some had small children with them. All were there for the same reason

I was—to spend a few minutes with someone who had been detained. Who might be deported. Amelia and I locked eyes. I wondered if she and everyone else could hear my heart pounding.

At the side of the room, a door opened. Prisoners entered in single file behind guards. All wore orange jumpsuits. Amelia and I rose in anticipation of finding Papi. *One inmate. Two. Seven. Ten.* Loved ones reunited and hugged, settling in to talk as we continued to wait. At last, after about thirty men had come in, I spotted Papi.

I hardly recognized him. His chin and neck were covered in stubble, and he looked thin. His hair was unkempt, his teeth yellow. His smart, observant eyes looked wary. I saw the look of despair. Months before, in that lawyer's empty office, I'd seen my father at his most powerless. This was worse.

We hugged tightly. "Forgive me," he told me once he'd let me go. "I don't have any toothpaste in here." My father, so meticulous about hygiene, was self-conscious of his breath and appearance. He cupped his hand over his mouth in shame.

I glanced around nervously, unsure of what to say.

"How are you, *hija*?" Papi asked, to break the ice. I started to cry. "Don't cry," he told me. I wanted to hug him again, but another one of the prison rules was limited contact. "We talked about this," he told me. "You knew this could happen."

A shot of anger surged through me, which caught

me by surprise. Sure, I'd been aware I could lose him and Mami. Maybe. One day. But after years of no issues with Immigration Services, I'd been lulled into thinking we might just be safe. I'd convinced myself that if it were going to happen, it already would have. Then without warning, reality socked me in the face. I'm not sure *any* preparation could have helped lessen the sting.

"Have you been keeping up with your schoolwork?" Papi asked.

"Yes," I said, gripping the edges of the hard plastic chair so tightly that my knuckles turned white. Small talk was easier than saying *good-bye*, though. I wanted to avoid the inevitable truth: that we'd soon be forced apart.

"Have you been eating?" my father asked.

I looked over at Amelia. "Yes, everything's good, Papi," I told him. "I'm sharing a room with Gabriela. It's nice."

My dad turned to Amelia, who hadn't spoken a word. "Thank you so much for taking her in," he told her. Amelia nodded. "Maria and I appreciate it. We really do." He promised to send money from Colombia each month to cover my basic expenses.

Papi looked at the floor, then up at me. "I want you to know how badly I feel about all of this," he told me.

Near the end of the visit, my father stood, placed his hands gently on my shoulders, and leaned as close as he could to my right ear. "*Te amo*," he whispered. "I love you. *Se fuerte.*

Be strong. Don't forget that." He kissed my forehead quickly, before the guards could call him out for getting too close.

A bell rang. Time was up. All the inmates stood. "No, Papi!" I called out. He shushed me with a gentle hand gesture. Watching my daddy, my beach bud, my friend walk away in that orange jumpsuit was one of the hardest moments I have ever endured.

The ride home was silent. I glowered at the freeway out the window, recalling the years of worry my family had spent fearing arrest. I now wished we'd set aside the anxiety and instead simply savored our time together. All that worrying hadn't changed anything. If there was to be no happily ever after for my family, then we should've just lived as happily as we could have while we were still together.

Here's how I'd describe the women's prison waiting room: Hot. Crowded. Musty. Charming, right? Metal chairs lined the cement walls. A teenage mom tried to calm down her screaming baby; two seats over from her, an old man dozed off with his cane at his side. No one spoke. Amelia leaned toward me.

"You ready, hon?" she asked.

"I guess," I said, although I knew that wasn't true. I don't think you're ever actually *ready* to see your own mom locked up. And definitely not when you may never see her again. But I couldn't say that out loud.

The guard, a tall black man with dreads, lumbered into the doorway. "Ladies and gentlemen," he announced in a Jamaican accent, "no cell phones are permitted in the visitation area with the detainees," he said.

The detainees. His words hung there, thick and heavy.

Weeks earlier, my mami had simply been the loving mother who combed my long black hair into a ponytail. The mom who made sure I brushed my teeth and finished my homework. Then in one afternoon, Mami had been suddenly labeled a prisoner. A "detainee." And in less than one hour, she'd be forced out of the country.

We made our way down a hall and into a second waiting area, which was somehow even more depressing than the first. The guard rounded the corner into the room. "When you hear your name," he barked, "please stand and follow me." I held my breath. Ten names in, I heard what I'd been listening for but dreading: "Diane Guerrero," he announced. Amelia and I took our places among the others and filed out behind the guard. Halfway down the hall hung a sign: INMATE VISITATION AREA. The guard swung a steel door open. He motioned for us to walk through.

Under fluorescent lights, about twenty inmates in orange jumpsuits sat lined up in booths behind a giant plastic barrier. Every booth had an old-school phone in its upper left-hand corner. Five or six guards milled around, just watching. I scanned the row. There, in the middle, was Mami. I walked across the linoleum and slid into the chair facing her. Amelia reached up and handed me the phone.

In the weeks since her arrest, Mami's beautiful face had aged twenty years. She seemed tired and frail, like she hadn't slept for days. I'd never seen her so skinny. Her eyes were red; her usually golden skin was pale. Her wrists were hand-cuffed together and resting in the lap of her orange jumpsuit. A guard on her side of the barrier placed the phone in her hands. She lifted it to her ear.

"Hello, my princess," she said. Her voice was so soft that I almost couldn't hear her. "How are you?"

My fingers trembled as I stared at her through the scratched plastic. "I'm okay," I said. I bit down on my lip to keep the tears from escaping. It didn't work. "I'm, uh— I'm fine," I stammered.

Mami dropped her head. "Don't cry, baby," she said, just as Papi had. Her own eyes betrayed her, though. They, too, were shiny with tears. "Please don't cry. I'm really sorry about this whole thing. I'm so sorry, Diane."

She didn't mean for her words to sting, but they did. She was sorry. My dad was sorry. The whole world was sorry. But none of it changed my situation. None of it altered the fact that, by dusk, they would be gone and my childhood would be over.

My mother looked intently at me. "What are you going to do, Diane?"

It was a big question for a mother to ask her child. But I knew my answer. I sat forward in my chair. "I'm staying, Mami," I said. "I've gotta stay."

I'd somehow always known I'd remain. What would I do in Colombia, a place I'd never even been to? What kind of life could I have in a nation so poor that my parents had risked everything to escape?

"You see that guy?" My mother tilted her head toward a Dominican-looking guard on my side of the plastic. He must've felt us staring, because he looked over at us. "You know what he told me?" she asked.

"What?" I said.

She moved the receiver as close to her mouth as she could. "He said Immigration only goes after people if they get a tip."

"What do you mean?"

"I mean they're not going around looking for random janitors," she told me. "Someone had to inform them about us."

I gazed at her. "But who would've done that?"

"I don't know for sure," she told me. She inhaled and then slowly released her breath. "That's why you've gotta watch your back," she said. "Be very careful, Diane."

The face of our unsympathetic neighbor flashed before my eyes. Could it be? Who would do this to us? I started to cry—and this time I didn't hold back. Enormous tears rolled down my cheeks and dripped from my chin. I wiped my face with the edge of my T-shirt. Amelia, who'd been standing beside me the whole time, rubbed my back. The Dominican guard walked in our direction.

"Are you her daughter?" he asked me. I nodded my head yes.

"It's okay, sweetheart," he said. "We're not going to hurt your mom."

That made me cry even louder. "So why does she have to wear those handcuffs?" I shouted, thrusting my chin toward Mami's sore wrists. "Can't you take them off? She's not going to do anything!" Several people looked over at me.

"I'm sorry, but she has to have those on," he told me. "That's the rules."

Soon after, a guard on my mother's side yelled, "Wrap it up! Five minutes!" Mami scooted to the edge of her stool and put her face right up to the barrier.

"I love you, honey," she whispered. She paused, stared down at the floor, and then looked back at me. "Never forget that. I'm so proud of you. Be a good girl, okay?"

I let go of the receiver and cupped my hands over my eyes. There were so many things I needed to tell her, so many words I'd stored away. I wanted to stand up and scream, "My mother is not a criminal! Don't you people understand? You've got the wrong family! Please—let her go!" But all I could do was wail. "Bye, Mami," I said between sobs. "Good-bye."

Our time was up.

Amelia held my hand while we walked back down the corridor. "This isn't the end for you, Diane," she said, to reassure me. But it felt like the end. As devastated as I was for my mom, I was even more scared for myself. She and my dad were returning to their Colombian home. I was stepping into a future I'd prayed would never come. Already I felt so alone.

Outside in the parking lot, Amelia tried to remember where she'd parked her car. Suddenly, we saw a white police van pull up. Amelia and I exchanged a look. Seconds later, two guards herded some inmates out onto the curb. My mother was among them. She turned and caught a glimpse of me. She froze. I could tell she wanted to say something, to run to me. But before she could make a move, a guard rushed her into the van. "Let's go!" he snapped.

The van's engine rumbled. From her seat in the rear, Mami twisted herself around so she could see me through the bars on the windows. She was trying to tell me something, but I couldn't figure out what it was. Then all at once, I understood. "I love you," she was mouthing. "I love you. I love you. I love you." She repeated the three words until the van turned from the lot and disappeared.

The next day, I'd begin a new life, one uncertain and frightening. A makeshift family. A different home. A path I'd prayed so hard that I'd never end up taking. My mother's warning, the haunting admonition, echoed through me. *Be careful. Be careful. Be careful.*

Me and Gaby, sophomore year, in the BAA music room. This picture hung all year in our humanities teacher's room. As you can see, some hater vandalized it. Joke's on you, pahtna!

With my cousin Andres on my fifteenth-birthday vacation to Cartagena, Colombia

11
SECOND FAMILY

The summer I lost my parents, it was the strangest kind of heartache. No friends gathered to grieve. No flowers were sent. No memorial service was planned. And yet the two people I'd cherished most were gone. Not gone from the world itself, but gone from me.

I didn't get to see Papi the afternoon he was deported. Immigration officials hadn't given us a heads-up, and since it happened in the middle of a weekday, Amelia couldn't leave work. As much as I wanted to cling to him, in a way it was simpler to miss the final meeting, to avoid seeing him suffer.

I hadn't expected a fairy-tale ending, but I hadn't expected one so abrupt, either. There had been no closure. Seeing my parents with their spirits broken, their heads dropped, had brought almost more sorrow than my heart could hold. But the more I lingered in the grief, the less I could function. So a little at a time, I strived to create a so-called new normal. At fourteen, I knew that I needed to look ahead.

Amelia was wonderful to me. She, Gabriela, and her other two children, both of whom were in their twenties, made me feel like part of the family. They were beyond hospitable—and yet I knew I was a guest. "*Mi casa es su casa*," any polite Latino host will tell you. But I had this nagging fear that I might do something to get myself thrown out. So I, aware of the major sacrifice she was making to have me there, went out of my way to respect boundaries.

Perfect example: I took up as little space as possible. I stuffed my few belongings into Gaby's bottom drawers and one closet corner. I stored my toiletries inside a travel bag rather than on the sink top or in the shower. With five people in the house, things were already cramped. I didn't want to make Amelia or her children regret her choice to take me in. I also recognized how much responsibility she had as a single working parent. I did all I could to lighten her load. Without her having to ask, I vacuumed and dusted. Each time I used a plate, I washed it, dried it, and put it in the cabinet. Between meals, Gabriela would sometimes grab a snack from the fridge; I got Amelia's permission before I ate anything. "You know," Gabriela would tease me, "you don't have to ask my mom *every* time."

I was so mindful of not rocking the boat that you can

imagine how upset I was if I somehow did. Several weeks into my stay, Gabriela pulled me aside.

"Um, can I talk to you for a sec?" she asked.

"Sure," I said. My throat tightened. Was I getting the boot?

"I know you don't mean for this to happen," she continued, "but my sister has been finding a lot of your hair in the bathroom."

I wrinkled my forehead. "*My* hair?"

"Yep," she answered. "It sheds. Before you leave the bathroom, can you please clean it up?"

"I'm so sorry, Gabriela. I promise I'll do that," I said, the tears welling up.

From then on, I was careful about my hair. After untangling my straight, long black mane, I'd thoroughly wipe down the sink and pick up every. Single. Strand.

Papi sent money, as promised. If Amelia gave me a few dollars, I held on to it; I could make fifty bucks last for weeks. I loved being able to buy small things for myself, like juice or pizza or tampons. I was smart and careful about my purchases. I couldn't wait to turn sixteen so I could get a job. Financial independence was the goal. While kids my age were talking about fashion or giggling about crushes, I was figuring out how I could make it on my own. My parents' deportation had made a mini adult of me.

I craved my family—my roots, the people who had raised

me and witnessed me from day one. I longed for the simplest experiences: watching a silly movie with Papi. Or Mami making me hot tea when I had cramps. I missed my parents most on one night in particular—spring fest. I'd nearly decided to pull out of the duet because I was so shaken up, but I owed it to myself to go out there and rock it. Mr. Stewart, Damien, and I had worked hard. It would've been a shame to let our song go unsung.

The night of the concert rolled around. Amelia and Gabriela came to support me; so did Sabrina and her mom, Eva. "Dude, you're going to be fantastic," Gabriela told me before I went backstage. "We'll be cheering you on."

Everyone had a part; there were students of opera, jazz, classical, and chamber music. Our duet was at the end of the show. Mr. Stewart gave Damien and me our cue, and we strode to our microphones. I peered out across the audience. There was a sea of parents and siblings. Teachers and administrators. People from the community. Even as I was about to perform, I was pinching myself that I'd been chosen.

Damien delivered his opening lines beautifully. Then came my cue. I closed my eyes, letting the audience fall away and tuning in to the music. "'In a world that's moving too fast,'" I sang softly. "'In a world where nothing can last, I will hold you . . . I will hold you.'" My voice shook with nerves. And the words I'd practiced over and over now suddenly seemed new. Different. Emotional. "'So stay with me and hold me tight,'" we sang in unison. "'And dance with me like it's the last night of the world.'"

The piece ended with perfect harmony (if I do say so myself), and the room erupted in applause. Damien and I linked arms and bowed. I peered out again over the scores of faces, praying that, by some miracle, I'd spot Mami and Papi. Amid the bright lights and magic of that stage, the impossible seemed possible, even for the briefest of moments.

Growing up, my parents played the music and prepared the foods of their homeland. They told Eric and me stories from their childhoods. We talked frequently to our loving aunts, uncles, and cousins on the phone; a few even visited Boston. So over the years, though I'd never visited Palmira, Colombia, in a way, I felt like I'd been a dozen times. In July 2001, two months after my parents' arrest and just after their departure, Papi arranged for me to spend a month there.

In the days leading up to my trip, I was as excited as I was nervous. How would it feel to see my parents again? What would their living conditions be? And was it safe there? As soon as my relatives heard I was coming, they began putting in requests for me to bring American gifts, such as Victoria's Secret lotion and Snickers candy bars. Papi warned me to keep a close eye on my bags.

A week before takeoff, Papi admitted some tough news to me. "Your mother and I have decided to separate," he said.

I pressed the phone closer to my ear. My heartbeat sped up. "What are you talking about, Papi?"

"We're no longer speaking to each other," he said. "When you come here, you can spend time with each of us. But don't expect us to do things together."

I nearly dropped the phone. All the bickering, the blaming each other for their circumstances, had threatened my parents' relationship for years. Deportation was the final blow. Once in Colombia, they had gone their separate ways. Mami moved in with her brother; Papi stayed with his sister. They lived minutes away from each other, as they had growing up, but now they were worlds apart.

With a heavy heart, I set out for Palmira on the eve of my fifteenth birthday. "Be careful, and call me once you're there," Amelia told me as she dropped me off at Logan International Airport for the long flight.

Mami and Papi had told me they'd meet me in the airport lounge of Alfonso Bonilla Aragón in Cali, Colombia. Upon landing, I walked curiously out of the aircraft to find them. I couldn't help noticing a swell of music in the air. It grew louder with every step. I furrowed my brow. Was this what I thought it was? Yes—my mother had hired a full band to celebrate my arrival. Balloons, streamers, and a sign that read WELCOME TO COLOMBIA, DIANE! filled the waiting area. Members of my extended family and Mami's neighbors all cheered, called out my name, and snapped photos. So. Embarrassing. I met eyes with Mami and Papi, both of whom were waving madly at me. Astonished, I tried to put on a half smile. After all, it's not every day that you get serenaded. The whole thing was pretty funny. Well, sort of.

"You're here!" Mami shrieked. She rushed toward me with a hug. Papi stood aside as we embraced, and then he leaned in and kissed me on the forehead. "Hello, *chibola*," he said. "I'm glad you made it." I noticed that my parents didn't speak much to each other, but at least they'd made the effort to pick me up together, for my sake. Meanwhile, the band played on. People I didn't know pushed bouquets into my hands. Finally, we all made our way outside through the sliding doors.

First stop: a party at my aunt's place. My uncle drove Mami and me there. As you know by now, my mother can be chatty, but on this day, she was completely wound up. She hurled question after question at me. "How's Amelia?" she asked. Before I could answer, she was on to the next topic: "Did you bring the lotion and all the other gifts for the family? And how did spring fest turn out?"

I squinted through the car window, dazed and silent. It was humid in downtown Cali. Locals on bikes weaved in and out of traffic. Old, stylish cars, models I hadn't seen in America, honked and switched lanes without signaling. Teenagers strutted by in crop tops and skinny jeans. Music rang out from all directions. The entire scene was chaotic. Colorful. Wild.

Then on the road into Palmira, we saw throngs of bare-foot children begging. Some wandered up to our car and pleaded for money or food; many were juggling limes, trying to earn cash.

"Mami, why are there so many children on the streets?" I asked.

"Diane, they're homeless." My mother sighed.

"Where are their parents?" I asked.

"I don't know," she told me. My eyes filled with tears. I couldn't imagine what it would be like for a five- or seven-year-old child to be left on their own. In the States, of course I'd seen homeless people around, but I hadn't witnessed this kind of hardship. I was struck with a realization: This could have been my life.

We pulled up to my aunt's house. Excited relatives filed out of the front door to greet us. Among the faces, I saw Eric. I lit up.

"How are you, sis?" he said, picking me up and twirling me. "You're so *tall* now!" He looked different. Better. His face was clean-shaven, his complexion bright. During his first months in Colombia, he'd struggled, floating from one family member's home to the next. It had pained him to leave America without being granted the dignity he deserved. But he eventually found work as an English teacher. On the day of our reunion, he seemed happy.

I'd stay with Mami first. Both of my parents lived in tiny

adobe homes in working-class areas. In the United States, their neighborhoods would be considered quite poor. Many of the residents, for instance, had only cold water; you had to be wealthy to afford hot.

"Come on in," Mami said as we walked through the door of my uncle's three-bedroom house. "Make yourself comfortable." I rolled in my suitcase, set it aside, and began glancing around.

I was shocked at how my mother was living. The den was empty. With no money for a sofa, she used folding metal chairs to sit. In the kitchen, a washboard and bucket leaned near the sink. Mami had to clean her clothes by hand. With no AC or fan, she labored over the hot stove to prepare meals.

I followed my mother into a rear bedroom. There, she shared a tiny space with my young cousin. He slept on the top bunk, she on the bottom. Because she had no dresser, she lived from her bag—the one I'd hurriedly packed for her. She reached down, pulled out a coat from her luggage, and chuckled.

"So why'd you put *this* in here?" She smirked. "In this climate, I certainly didn't need a coat." I rolled my eyes. She went on to mention that I'd accidentally given her mismatched shoes. I knew my mother was half joking, but her complaining annoyed me. How was I supposed to know what to pack that night? Didn't she understand the stress I'd been under? "I did my best," I murmured. "At least you got a bag."

Here's the truth: I felt sorry for my mother. At the same

time, I blamed her for our predicament. By reopening the case in New Jersey, she made herself vulnerable to deportation. I knew she did it because she wanted citizenship so badly, but it still made me angry. Even still, I blamed her for the less-than-cautious way in which she'd handled the situation. And I can't tell you how angry that made me.

I dealt with my resentment by going out a lot, mostly with other family. I'd clicked with three of my cousins, Andre, Felipe, and Lena; all were within a couple of years of my age.

"Wanna go out tonight?" Felipe would swing by and ask.

"Sure," I'd say, glancing at Mami's face to check with her. She didn't hold me back from having fun, even if it meant spending less time together.

With my cousins as my tour guides, I experienced a side of Colombia I loved. There, teens have more freedom than in America, so we'd be out for hours without even checking in at home. We ate, went to the movies, the park, the mall. We danced all night at salsa clubs. Even with its many issues, the country has this amazing energy, this irresistible vibrancy that draws you in.

From the moment I stepped off the plane, people were all over me. I felt like a celebrity. "Can Diane come over for lunch today?" one of Mami's brothers would call and ask. An hour later, the phone would ring with an additional invitation. Everywhere I went, people wanted to feed me, talk to me, hug me, dance with me, or introduce me to their friends and family. Why all the attention? Because others saw me as unique. I was this American girl who'd lived what many Colombians consider the dream life; and yet I was also connected to my Colombian roots. This combo made me uncommon. I appreciated all the fuss, but, to be honest, I was also overwhelmed by it.

My last two weeks were spent with Papi. His surroundings were as modest as Mami's, but he was chill about it. In fact, he was quiet overall and maybe a little down. At dusk, when the humidity had dropped, he'd often take me out biking. One evening as we returned, I struck up a conversation.

"Papi?" I asked.

"Yes, Diane," he said. "What is it?"

"Do you think someone turned you and Mami in?"

He paused. "What do you mean?" he asked.

"One of the guards at the detention center told Mami that someone probably snitched on you guys."

"I don't know, Diane," he said. He looked away from me. "And at this point," he went on, "I guess it doesn't matter. We're here now. There's not much I can do about it." We left the mystery at that.

On the Sunday of my last week, Papi surprised me. "I want to take you someplace special for your birthday," he said. "Just the two of us." In Latin cultures, turning fifteen is a big deal for a girl; it marks the beginning of womanhood. Years before, I'd told my parents I had no desire for a *quinceañera*, the traditional ceremony complete with white gloves and ball gowns. Not my thing. But I did want some kind of party, and, in fact, I'd already had three since I'd arrived in Colombia—one thrown by my mother, a second by my father's sister, and a third courtesy of my cousins. So when Papi told me he'd top all that off with a vacay, I was thrilled.

"Where are we going?" I asked.

"I'm taking you to Cartagena," he told me.

I raised my eyebrows. "Really, Papi?" I squealed. I'd heard that the historic city on the Caribbean coast was one of Colombia's most gorgeous.

"Yes, really," he said, laughing. "I used some of my savings to buy our tickets. We'll go this week."

I wasn't just excited; I was also grateful for Papi's generosity. Together, we strolled through the streets of Old Town, savored ceviche at a quaint restaurant, and watched the red-golden sunset over the silver waters. The getaway was perfect.

At the end of the month, both of my parents went to the airport to see me off. "Why don't you come live here?" Mami said. I didn't respond. As much as I relished certain things about the trip, I knew there was no life for me there. Papi stood quiet. In fact, he'd never said one way or the other whether he wanted me to move there. He knew I'd already made up my mind. I heard my call to board. I kissed each of them good-bye and set off for the one homeland I'd ever truly known.

Super emo. Wouldn't smile. Mouth full of metal. Sophomore year at BAA.

12

GROWING PAINS

Refreshed from my summer vacation, I began sopho-more year. I was no longer the new kid. Classes were better than ever, and I was excited about developing as a student and artist. That fall semester also came with a bonus: Gabriela became my classmate, switching into the theater department. The only thing better than being at Boston Arts was having a close friend there. By this time, Dana had moved to Florida with her family. Gabriela and I sometimes ran into Sabrina, but less frequently than before.

After that taste of freedom in Palmira, I returned ready to spread my social wings. At a movie theater near campus, a bunch of my friends and I would hang out after school. We'd snap photos of one another (the old-school kind that you have to get developed at Walgreens, LOL) and just be ridiculous.

That year, we were obsessed with John Leguizamo, the Colombian-American comedian and actor. Seeing a Latino in the spotlight meant the world to me. So you can imagine how excited we all were when he visited our campus. For months afterward, we'd entertain ourselves by reciting every joke the guy had told. It was the best time.

One evening that December, I called Amelia to ask for permission to go to the store down the street alone. I wanted to buy some colored pencils for an art project.

"Why don't you wait until later?" she said. "We'll be there shortly. Gabriela can go with you."

I persisted. She gave in. "Okay, but don't be gone for long."

I knew the route well. Gabriela and I passed the store every day on our way to school. I pressed the crosswalk button. The go signal appeared. So I looked both ways and began strolling across the street. When I was about halfway to the other side, a green Mazda swerved out in front of me and—*boom!*—crashed into the right side of my body. The driver, a young white woman, hurried from the driver's side and over to me. I lay sprawled out on the pavement, moaning.

"Miss! Miss!" the lady screamed. "What were you doing crossing the street like that?" She reached down and took my hand. With her help, I slowly stood. My knees were bloody, and my right arm throbbed.

"Let me call nine-one-one," she said, searching for her phone. I grabbed her arm. "Please don't!" I screamed. "I'm fine!"

"But, miss," she said, "you're hurt!"

"Go, go, go!" I begged, tears flooding my face. "I'm okay!"

You have to understand. I had one thought on my mind: *Do not cause any trouble.* If the police showed up, they might realize my parents had been deported and throw me in the foster care situation I so dreaded. I planned to stay as far under the radar as my family had always been. On top of that, I refused to hassle Amelia. Rather than calling for help, I hobbled home, cleaned myself up, and came up with a story about how I'd hurt myself.

"Oh my God, what happened?" Amelia said the second she opened the door and saw me in bandages. She put her groceries on the counter and rushed to my side of the sofa.

"Oh, it's nothing," I lied. "I fell down the stairs at school."

"Why didn't you tell me?" she gasped. "Are you okay?"

"I'm fine," I assured her. "It's not a big deal."

But of course, Amelia insisted on taking me to the ER to be checked. Once there, doctors discovered that I'd cracked my wrist. Hours later, and a few weeks before Christmas, I left the hospital in a cast I'd have to wear for six weeks. I spent the final days of 2001 recovering from a broken arm, regretting the deep fracture in my family, and hoping I'd wake up to discover that the last few months had been only a bad dream.

"Hello, Diane?"

"Hi, Papi," I said. "What is it?"

He paused. "I got a call from Amelia today," he said.

"You did?" I asked. My pulse quickened. "Everything okay?"

He stopped. "She cannot have you there any longer."

I got up from the couch and walked out toward the balcony to get some privacy. "But . . . I mean . . . why?" I stammered.

"Because her oldest daughter just found out that she's pregnant," he told me. "And with the baby coming, there's not enough room for you."

But Gabriela's sister didn't *look* pregnant. What else could it be? My mind scrambled to think what I might have done to cause this. Things seemed pretty perfect between Gabriela and me, but earlier that week we had argued: nothing major, just a tiff between friends. I must've recently slacked on my chores without realizing. I pressed my father for more information.

"So did I do something wrong?" I asked. My voice shook. "Are they upset with me about something?"

"No, *mija*," he told me. "It's not about anything you did. Not at all. It's only because the house is too small. Amelia was only supposed to have you there for a few months. You've now been with her for over a year."

"So what am I gonna do?" I asked. My eyes welled up with tears. Amelia and Gabriela had become family to me. I didn't want to be alone again, as I had been that night hiding under the bed.

"Well, I've spoken to Sabrina's parents. They said that they'll take you in," he assured me, emphasizing that it would all be okay.

Upon the mention of my pal's name, a weight lifted from my shoulders. But tears poured out nonetheless. I. Did. Not. Want. To. Move. AGAIN. It sucked. Going from place to place meant that at a moment's notice, I could be asked to leave. That's the reality when your own family isn't there to anchor you.

Amelia heard me sniffling and knew why. She sidled up next to where I sat on the balcony and placed her hand on my shoulder. "I just want you to know something, Diane," she said softly. "You didn't do anything wrong. My daughter is having a baby. That's it. That's the only reason."

So it wasn't me? I'd done my dishes enough, collected my hair, been a good girl? I wiped the tears from my face. From the compassion in her eyes, I knew she was sincere. I was grateful that Papi had lined up my next move, and what better move than with my homie Sabrina and her parents, Eva and Donald. They'd come from Colombia years earlier, been granted citizenship, and owned their home. Like with Gabriela, we'd been friends for so long that I'd practically grown up there.

I dialed Sabrina. "Hey, guess what?" I said, trying to seem upbeat.

"What?" she said.

"I'm coming to your place," I told her.

She giggled and exclaimed, "I know! My mother told me. But I couldn't say anything to you about it yet."

A week later, I packed up. Gabriela helped me gather my things and saw me off. "Sorry, dude," she told me. "I hate to see you go." Amelia placed my bag into her trunk and drove me to Sabrina's home, which was in our old stomping grounds. Sabrina and her parents welcomed me warmly. "Come on in," said her mother, Eva. "You'll be in Sabrina's room." And that's how the summer before my junior year began. Another house. A new family.

Next big change: I got a job. Sabrina had been working at iParty, this party supply store in West Roxbury. They sold everything, from streamers, balloons, and Halloween costumes to paper plates and cups. A few weeks later, as the fall semester got under way, Sabrina got me a gig as a cashier at $5.15 an hour, minimum wage then. I put in twenty hours a week, mainly on weekends and a couple of days after school. If our shifts overlapped, we would drive together and sing to the radio.

The new job was a lot to juggle with my studies, but it was worth it to me. It meant I didn't have to depend on anyone. And bonus: If I wanted a cute shirt from H&M or a tube of lipstick—*ka-ching!*—I could buy it myself.

Maybe it's dorky to be so enthusiastic about school, but I loved it. And during the fall of my junior year, Boston

Arts got even better. Ms. Jackson, this excellent teacher in the music department, inspired me, picking up where Mr. Stewart left off. With her encouragement, I began exploring jazz greats like Miles Davis, Nina Simone, and my favorite, Sarah Vaughan. She, like so many women of color before, broke the ceiling for putting our talents in the spotlight. Healing power lived in her music. I felt less alone knowing these performers could take their pain and channel it into their art. They had created something beautiful from hardship. I wanted to one day do the same.

Having enthusiasm isn't the same thing as having confidence, though. I still had my doubts and insecurities. Aside from that duet at spring fest, I'd stuck to being a member of the chorus. It was safer. I didn't want to seem like a show-off. Some of the other kids at BAA were very talented—I'm talking Adele pipes. Their "sound" seemed perfect. I questioned my own singing voice for not sounding like theirs; I didn't yet have the confidence to appreciate that sounding different was what made me unique.

Another worry nagged at me: If I pursued a career in the arts, how would I pay my bills? Could I support myself once I was eighteen and on my own? The dreams I'd had since childhood burned brightly inside of me. I was still the same girl who'd fantasized of taking on Broadway. Yet as graduation inched closer, I got less and less convinced that I had the chops to make it.

Me on graduation day from BAA. Of course, I thought I was the only one graduating.

Senior recital day with friends from the music department at BAA

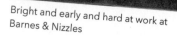

Bright and early and hard at work at Barnes & Nizzles

13

BUTTERFLY

Buried beneath all my work and activities was a broken heart. I became a classic avoider, talking to my mother and father only if there was no way out of it. Whenever Eva handed me the phone and said, "Your mom wants to speak to you," I'd think, *Here we go again.*

Mami's life was one never-ending *telenovela*, complete with full-length episodes of drama, hardship, and agony. She'd tell me how this aunt or uncle had lost a job, how someone had been mugged on the way to the grocery store, and, of course, how much she wanted us all to be together again.

So did I; I just saw no point in rehashing it. "Okay, Mami, I've gotta go," I'd say to rush her off the line. It was my sixteen-year-old way of shouting, "I can't deal with this anymore!"

Meanwhile, I'd lost touch with another family member. One weekend, walking through a park in town, I heard someone cry out, "Aunt Diane! Aunt Diane!" *Me*, Diane? I whirled around. There, running toward me, was my niece, Erica. The world stopped for a moment. In the middle of the loud music, the screams, the children begging their mothers for cotton candy, I stood there dazed. She was about seven and had gotten so much taller. How quickly time was passing!

"How are you, sweetie?" I asked, scooping her up in a big hug.

"I miss you!" she squealed.

"I know," I said, still stunned. "Me too."

If I was struggling at my age with my family's deportation, it must have been crushing for her. She'd lost her father and two grandparents, all before her fifth birthday. Although the circumstances were out of my control, I felt like I'd abandoned Erica. Just thinking about that hurt. Following our reunion in the park, Gloria occasionally brought my niece to Sabrina's place. But between her busy schedule as a single parent and all my work and responsibilities, our visits petered out.

By that spring, my parents had taken to leaving angry messages on my voice mail; that's how infrequently I'd reached out to them. I loved and missed them as much as they did me, but—to put it simply—talking to them hurt. It was a reminder of everything I was desperate to forget.

"Please come here, sweetie," Mami would weep. "I need to see you."

That's how my second trip to Colombia came about, during the summer after my junior year. The trip was a blur. I may have gone there to spend time with my folks, but I spent most of my time chilling with my cousins—dancing at salsa clubs and basically having a blast. It was my chance to let loose, to set aside the pressure of being a good girl, a perfect houseguest. Every weekend, we'd camp, make fires, play in the pool, and laugh all night.

I brought the party back to Boston with me—senior year is when I blossomed socially. My self-doubts hadn't magically melted away (yeah, right), but I was becoming surer of myself. Maybe it was the fact that I'd saved up some money, which gave me a sense of power. Or maybe it was just growing up.

I threw myself into extracurriculars. One of my favorites was the literary magazine called *SlateBlue*; Gabriela, several other students, and I would gather our classmates' short stories and poetry and choose the best to include in an annual collection. In class and out, I was learning to express my opinions. Reading books by great thinkers, especially Simone de Beauvoir and many other incredible feminists, gave me confidence in my own voice and opinions. And rather than heading straight home after work, I wanted to have a life. I started hanging with my friends on the weekends, socializing and going to dinner. We may not have had much money, but we found ways to rock whatever we did and make it fun.

And yet here's the funny thing: As much hurt and frustration as I held inside me deep down, I never went buck wild or got super-rebellious. When my classmates who had their parents here would get into trouble for no reason, I thought it was ridiculous. That probably seems judgmental, but I couldn't understand it. They had so many great things going for them and yet were willing to ruin it. In a way, not having Mami and Papi close led me to give myself rules and maintain good behavior.

Like my parents before me, I was careful and law-abiding out of necessity. First, out of fear of getting found by authorities, who would have me put into foster care. Second, because if my parents had a chance of coming back, it would be through me as their lifeline. And third, I didn't have people to bail me out. My friends who took care of me were loving and generous, but they had their own issues and expenses to deal with. I didn't want to be a burden. I wanted to show people that even without my family here, I could remain on track.

In the fall, my friend Sophia, a theater major and incredibly talented poet, got me in at the Barnes & Noble Café in the Prudential Center. She and my girl Sasha were always talking about how much they loved it there. Once I got hired, the three of us became our own little club. We usually worked from 5:00 p.m. to close, or at the crack of dawn on weekends, and we joked around the whole time. So much fun. Even work can be joyful if you've got your friends with you.

My spring semester, I was in the dopest ensemble in school—rhythm and voice. The whole semester was all about preparing for senior recital, the final evaluation. We got to choose our own songs. I picked "Funny Honey" from *Chicago*, a classical French piece, my favorite Sarah Vaughan rendition, and a few other numbers. Two afternoons a week, a voice coach came in to work with us one-on-one. I spent literally hours rehearsing. While brewing coffee at Barnes, I was humming and tapping my toes. I intended to be ready.

When I wasn't whipping up cappuccinos or belting in the music room, I was hitting the books hard and prepping for SATs. With only months left until graduation, it was time to figure out my path—and I was zigzagging all over the place. I really wanted to do work that made some kind of difference—but what? Maybe I could study political science and communication and be a television news anchor? There was one thing I did know for sure: I'd apply to college. The staff at BAA had ingrained that in me from the get-go.

In March, many of my classmates began receiving acceptance letters from universities all over the country. I hadn't yet applied. Why? Because I was terrified that I wouldn't get in. "It's not too late," my guidance counselor, Mr. McCaffrey, told me. "I can help you with the paperwork."

I applied to five programs in New England—all women's colleges. I figured that with no boys to distract me, I'd be able to focus. As hard as I'd worked to get good grades throughout high school, though, my GPA was average, not stellar. My expectations for getting in were not high.

To my delight, that April, I got called in for an interview at my top school: Regis College, a private Roman Catholic university a few miles outside of downtown Boston. Eva drove me to the campus—and did I mention it was gorgeous? Lush, green lawns. Massive trees. Historic brick buildings. That fantasy of living in a fancy suburban town had come to life. I was enthralled by the classes I sat in on. Maybe I could make a path for myself there, grow as a student, and make friends. And the teachers, some of whom were nuns, seemed to care about the students. Things were looking up.

I knew what I'd come there to do: show them what I was made of. Wearing a cute dress and my fake pearls, I made my case to the admissions team as strongly as I could. "I would be a great addition to your school," I told them passionately. "If you give me this opportunity, I will do everything possible to excel." A month later—*boom shakalaka*—I was accepted. I was going to college!

It didn't hurt that Regis offered me a financial-aid package that covered most of my first-year costs. I did have a moment of panic, however, when I realized I'd still have to take out some loans in order to pay the rest of the fees. I didn't understand a lot of what I signed up for when I took out those school loans—I signed and hoped for the best.

A couple of weeks before the end of the term, my senior recital came around. I arose early that morning to warm up my voice with some scales. I wore a beautiful pink strapless dress, one I'd picked out at Forever 21, and pink flowers in my hair from my other favorite "designer," H&M. I wore my mother's shawl as a good-luck charm; I swear I could still smell her perfume on it.

"You ready?" asked Ms. Jackson that morning, with a smile that told me she knew I was.

"Yes," I replied with assurance.

The next hour was one of the most special of my life. As I sang the pieces I'd worked so hard on, the music transported me far away, to a place where sorrow and heartache and misery don't exist. I gave in to the feeling, allowing it to carry me off. I ended with a jazz standard called "Poor Butterfly." It's about this Japanese woman enchanted by an American man who never returns to be with her. I'd chosen it because it struck a powerful chord in me. The abandonment. The hoping and waiting and yearning for something that doesn't happen.

"'Poor butterfly,'" I sang. "'. . . The moments pass into hours, the hours pass into years. And as she smiles through her tears, she murmurs low.'"

At the end of my concert, the room went wild. Ms. Jackson

and the other teachers all stood and clapped, a long round of applause that meant more to me than any I've received since. Sabrina, Eva, Gabriela, and Amelia all sat beaming and clapping in the front row. I was so appreciative of their support, awed by my luck. I had done it, and it felt so good. It took courage for me to put my voice on display, to let myself be seen and heard as I am. Succeeding takes courage—the first step is putting yourself out there. And for once, I was not afraid. There in the auditorium, I was surrounded by an overwhelming spirit of love and support.

Think about all the big things that happen between ages fourteen and eighteen, how we change and develop and step into our personalities. Proms. Recitals. Birthdays. Graduation. At the end of my years at Boston Arts, I was already a little adult. I'd grown from that girl once frightened and shivering under a bed to a poised young woman, a butterfly, ready to spread my wings and navigate my life. And my parents, as deeply as they wished otherwise, hadn't been there to witness any of the transformation.

Sophomore year at Regis College. The orientation leaders and me.

14

ANOTHER WORLD

The good news: I graduated high school and got into college! The bad news: The second I stepped onto campus, I felt like a total outcast. Sure, Regis was even more stunning in fall than it had been in spring, buzzing with that fresh back-to-school energy. But after that memorable recital, I kept thinking: *Why didn't I have the guts to try for a conservatory?*

I missed my crew, especially Gabriela, who'd enrolled in Pine Manor College, and Sabrina, who was attending beauty school to become a hairdresser. The girls and their moms all dropped me off in my dorm room a week ahead of the fall semester. "You always have a spot in our house," Eva assured me as we hugged good-bye through tears. "You can visit anytime."

But there I was. Right away, I had to make a huge adjustment to—how shall I put this?—hoity-toity suburban white girls. I officially felt like a "minority." Where were my people? The artsy weirdos. The immigrants and people of color. The outsiders who banded together to make a beautiful community. There were also some Asian, black, and brown girls, but not nearly as many as I was used to.

Luckily, I immediately clicked with my roommate, Adrienne, this gorgeous girl with auburn hair and green eyes. She'd been raised in a hippie-dippie community in the Berkshires. When she hung a *Les Misérables* poster over her bed, I knew she was my kind of roomie. Creative. Earthy. Cool.

During freshman year, I chose political science and communications as my major. The topics of race and culture were part of my curriculum. I was hungry to educate myself, to learn all about different worldviews. I read voraciously. Plato. Niccolò Machiavelli. Jean-Jacques Rousseau. I'd get so attached to whatever I was reading that I'd switch my view. Here's the thing: I wasn't simply reading. I was also carving out a belief system. An identity. A place to fit in as a Latina and a woman and a Millennial.

The more I learned about the world, the more complicated I realized it was. The way different cultures and people intersected and diverged was like an endlessly layered riddle. My classmates rarely matched my enthusiasm, though. Those around me were from communities where my reality—as the child of immigrants—wasn't part of their conversation. They paid little attention to the existence of undocumented workers—because they didn't have to. My family's struggle to remain in America had defined my childhood, yet immigration wasn't even a blip on their radars. Equal rights didn't seem to matter to them, because their rights were already secured.

Here was a strange paradox: While on one hand I stood out for looking "different" and being a first-generation American, on the other I was also treated as invisible—my history and background were barely treated as worthy of discussion. My peers had no idea what I'd been through. And it made me furious.

"Where do your parents live? When are they visiting you?" people asked me. Snort. *As if I'd tell you*, I thought. "They're retired," I'd say. Or "They returned to Colombia to run their own business." If anyone pressed the point, I quickly changed the subject. I was ready to turn the page on the "poor Diane" story.

Summer break: the time when my peers traded their studies for, say, a Tuscan vacation or a fancy internship. For me, the off-season meant panic mode. Where would I go? What would I do? How could I earn money? I wanted to be independent, to not have to rely on Eva to take me in. And so, at the end of my freshman year, I became an orientation leader, which meant I gave tours to visiting students and—bingo—stayed in the dorms for free during June, July, and August.

Holidays were tricky as well. While others were decking the halls, I was stressing about where to lay my head. Finally, with the help of Gabriela's sister, I landed a ticket to Colombia for Christmas 2005—don't worry, I paid her back promptly!

Just recalling Christmas in Colombia makes me feel warm. I'd heard about its holiday magic from my family. The stories didn't come close to the experience itself, though. The country bursts into celebration. There were parties all over the place and hundreds of twinkling lights. Music and fireworks filled the air. People went from house to house, singing and reciting verses during La Novena—like caroling or wassailing. We sang "Silent Night" and the traditional "Los Pastores de Belén." The sounds, the sights, the taste of *sabajón*, a Colombian-style eggnog—it all brought the season to life.

Mami and I exchanged gifts. I brought her the usual items on her list: lotion, perfume, makeup. Early that Christmas morning, before I'd gotten out of bed, she came into my room and handed me a package. My eyes lit up.

"Open it," she said. I peeled off the pink tissue paper. Inside, I found a stack of seven underwear, one in every color of the rainbow.

"Thank you," I whispered, reaching over to embrace her. It probably sounds like a small gift, but to me, getting cotton undies from my mom was a symbol of her care. It took me back to those days when I was six and nine and twelve, the years when Mami had been there to give me a personal item that often only a mother would buy for her daughter.

Leaving Colombia was always an emotional roller coaster. I dreaded saying good-bye to my folks, but I knew that my homeland was where I belonged. It was after that Christmas break that I firmly decided on my goal: After graduating, I would need to lock down a good job, save up, and hire a respectable, *real* attorney to bring my parents to the States. I didn't quite know *how* to do this, but the holiday was a reminder of how lonely I felt without Mami and Papi here. How much I needed them.

You'd think being homesick for my family would've prompted me to call them more regularly. It didn't. I would've given just about anything for them to be closer—and yet, I needed distance from the memory of losing them. Talking to them from so far away felt like a glaring reminder of it.

Avoidance was easier than looking at the distance between us in the face.

My classes were kicking my butt. As hard as I was working—and let me tell you, I stayed at the library until closing time on most days—I was still pulling only B's and C's. That's all good, but I wanted better, and I was making *such* an effort. It's not like I was partying or procrastinating. So I went in to talk to the school counselor.

"Have you been tested for a learning disability?" he asked. He recommended I take some tests. When the results came in, we discovered that—news flash!—since elementary school, I'd had ADD and mild dyslexia. What a revelation. I got on medication, requested extra time from my professors to complete exams, and sure enough, guess what? The A's began to roll in.

With my grades on the rise, I could focus on the next important issue: my lack of money. A trendy clothing store called Jasmine Sola was hiring, and I landed the gig. As I folded fancy items each evening, I drooled. I hadn't even been in the same room with $250 jeans before! Who had that much cash to drop on clothes? Oh, right—everyone in the store but me.

And so much for not being distracted by boys. One day on the job, I met a guy named David—he was handsome, with dark hair and a broad smile. That weekend, he took me out for a nice dinner. And then a second one the Friday after. And then a third the next week. Dating was pretty new to me. The handful of times I'd gone out in high school, the dude and I would chill with a group at the movies or McDonald's. This was different. David would call ahead, choose a restaurant, and then swing by my dorm to pick me up. We began seeing each other almost every weekend, and within a couple of months, he and I were officially together. I felt like a real grown-up. And yes—I made the dean's list that semester.

By the end of sophomore year, I'd at last broken my silence with my roommate Adrienne. She'd come back to our room one evening to find me bawling. She dropped her bag at the door to come and sit at the foot of my bed. Seconds later, my story came blustering out. From then on, I had my roommate's support and trusted her with my secret. But other people? Forget it. I still wouldn't tell a soul about my background.

In my junior year, I took the opportunity to study abroad at Regis's partner school in London. The Westminster campus was straight out of Hogwarts, complete with cobblestone streets and buildings that were centuries old. Adrienne, our friend Jennifer, and I shared a fancy-looking suite with a balcony overlooking a tree-lined courtyard. The way I saw it, being far away was my opportunity to become someone else. Like a secret agent, I could take on a new identity in a new place.

During my entire three months away, I talked to Mami and Papi only twice. In the second of those calls, Mami dropped some news. "I'm moving to Madrid," she said. "I need to start over somewhere new." A few years previously, her brother had moved to Spain for work; he encouraged her to join him there. I was surprised that Mami had made that decision without consulting me. Then again, I hadn't given her much of a chance to with my recent invisibility-cloak act.

After my adventure studying in London, I wasn't ready to return to Regis. I decided to spend the spring semester at American University in Washington, DC—another of my college's partner schools. I was studying foreign policy, which it turned out was *not* my jam; I preferred debating *this* country's social issues. I was no closer to figuring out my path. It's not like my parents or anyone else was giving me advice or asking, "Hey, Diane, what are you going to do with this degree?" I was just drifting—and praying I'd wind up going in the right direction.

Washington, DC, is a city full of energy and power. But studying there caused me trouble. I discovered (too late) that my costs there weren't covered by student loans. In desperation, I took out new, expensive loans and signed agreements without fully knowing what they were. The financial-aid office called me repeatedly to collect money I didn't have. What had I gotten myself into?

This is when things started to go downhill. I fell into a depression. I'm not talking about a little case of the blues. I'm talking about a dark, heavy fog that kept me in bed for days at a time. I skipped classes. Stopped socializing. My appetite disappeared. When Adrienne checked in on me, I reassured her I was fine so I could hang up. My whole body ached. My grades suffered. In a month, I went from excelling to nearly flunking out.

The combination of everything—being in debt, plummeting grades, and my relationship with David, which was constantly going up and down—overwhelmed me. I had a lot riding on this grand plan to make it through school, land a job, and bring my parents back here. None of it was falling into place. How could a school year that began on such an amazing high in London end up in the ditch? *Where did I go wrong?*

When I returned to Boston at the end of the semester, I moved in with David. Depression can take various forms, and mine showed up in new ways that summer and fall. I wanted to P.A.R.T.Y and—instead of dealing with my issues—stay out all night. The next afternoon, I'd awaken, dizzy and dry-mouthed, often too late to make it to class.

"Please call me!" Gabriela pleaded on my voice mail. "Please tell me you're okay." Sabrina, Eva, Amelia, and my aunt and uncle in New Jersey all rang as well, but I wouldn't call back. Adrienne once came by my apartment and banged on the door. "Hey, Diane!" she yelled out. "Are you in there?" I ignored her. I was too ashamed to discuss what was happening to me. So I tuned out my loved ones, and the more I rejected their help, the more isolated I became.

———

"Diane?"

My eyes fluttered open. David stood at my hospital bed, looking down at me. My head throbbed. The room was blurry. I noticed that my forearms were wrapped tightly in white bandages. A monitor at my left tracked my heartbeat. *Beep. Beep. Beep. Beep.*

"What happened?" I muttered. "Where am I?"

David pressed his lips together. "You tried to hurt yourself again," he said. He nodded toward my arms.

The cutting. The first time I'd harmed myself was in DC. One morning, I'd received the bad news about the cost of my student loans, and by that evening I was inconsolable. Reaching for a knife brought a strange relief. For a brief moment, the sharp physical pain replaced my emotional despair. But making myself bleed was not okay, and I knew it. If a friend told me she was doing it, I'd be worried about her. After that episode, I promised myself I'd never do that again. It frightened me.

My vow to myself didn't stick. As the sadness intensified, so did my desire to cut. Somehow, someway I needed to distract myself from this destructive urge. I'd scribble page after page about how lost I was. But my desire to hurt grew intense, and there I was again, holding a knife. At first, the wounds weren't noticeable. By the time I left DC, though, I had a collection of small scars.

To hide them, I wore long sleeves on hot days or I rubbed

makeup over them. But the gashes multiplied. One night David rushed me to the ER. That's how I wound up in that dinky hospital bed.

Just then, the curtain swung open. A nurse, a heavyset woman with wiry silver curls and glasses, marched in with a clipboard.

"You wanna talk about this, hon?" she said. I didn't respond. "We've got social workers on staff here. I'd like to set you up with one. Would you like that?"

"I guess so," I mumbled. "Whatever."

"It's up to you," she said, "Are your folks in the area?"

"Nope," I snapped.

"Well," she told me, "I really do hope you can get some help. You need it." I wouldn't admit it to her, but I knew she was right.

The hospital stay scared me straight for a couple of months. But like alcohol or drugs, cutting can be addictive. I tried to do it less, but I couldn't quite stop altogether. When I showed up for class, I'd catch people gawking at my arms, then quickly looking away. Their facial expressions said it all: *What is* wrong *with her?*

Papi and me at our favorite place in the whole world,
Nantasket Beach, Massachusetts

15

THE EDGE

As the holidays neared, the city buzzed with light, music, and joy. Crowds of families strolled gleefully along the boulevards.

Out in the world, I craved to crawl back under the covers. Here and there, I'd have a halfway-decent moment, a laugh, a little relief. But it was followed by a wave of gloom that knocked me back to my knees. I sleepwalked through my days, all of which looked exactly alike. Home. Work—I'd traded the fancy clothing store for a job bartending. Then back home with a heavy heart.

I was deep in debt, trying to cover the cost of my education. Between loans and credit cards, it seemed impossible to ever repay. I wished I knew someone who could give me guidance. Money is stressful, people! Voice mails from student-loan collectors poured in. My stomach flipped every time. *What do you want from me?* I wanted to shout. *I barely have enough for my next meal!*

One snowy, exhausting day after a long bartending shift, my phone rang. I could tell by the area code that it was a Colombian number. I let it go to voice mail. A half hour later, snuggled under the covers, I listened to the message.

"Diane, this is your papi," he said with a cracked voice. "Please call me. No one has heard from you in so long. You're not in trouble. I'm not going to yell at you. Please, *chibola*. I just want to know that you're okay." *Beep.*

I hadn't talked to either of my parents in forever. They rang all the time, of course, but like with the creditors, I ignored them.

From the outside, I realize that it seemed as if I didn't care about my mother and father, like I didn't miss them. Not at all. It broke my heart to know that they were hurting, and I missed them every single day. And yet the sadness that I felt hearing their voices was so deep and painful, that it actually felt worse than ignoring them did. I felt as if my own mother and father were foreigners to me, people I'd perhaps known in a former life but whom I did not recognize anymore. Facing that was devastating.

At 10:00 p.m., in spite of my dread, I began dialing my father's number. In the voice mail, he'd sounded frail. I wanted to check on him.

"Papi?" I said.

"*Hola, hija*—is that you?" he said sleepily.

"Yes, it's me," I said. "How are you?"

"I'm okay. It's great to hear from you. What's been happening?"

"Nothing much," I said, which was my standard answer. I couldn't bring myself to tell him about the depression. "How have you been? How's the family?"

He sighed. "Things are tough right now," he admitted. One of his brothers had been robbed. And he himself, who still hadn't been able to find work, was so low on money that he'd cut back to one meal a day. "But I don't want you to worry about me," he added. "I'll be okay." I had zero money, but I felt so badly for him that I offered to wire him some cash. He wouldn't hear of it. "Use it for school," he told me. "That's your focus right now."

We'd been on the line for fewer than five minutes, but I was nauseous with sadness and homesickness. "I love you, Papi," I told him, trying to end the call.

"I love you, too," he said. "I miss you so much. When can you come here?"

"I don't know. We'll see. But I'll call you later."

"You promise?"

"I promise," I said, but we both knew the truth. The second I put down the phone, I wailed.

At fourteen, I'd been able to push my feelings away and

focus on school, friends, and my creativity. Now in my early twenties, emotions bubbled back to the surface, impossible to ignore. I felt like that shy girl I once was, whose childhood had ended too soon. At the mention of my parents' names, I'd weep uncontrollably. School felt like a chore. Classmates peered curiously at my scarred arms. My grades sank. Keeping up with assignments was difficult—since I couldn't afford textbooks, I had to borrow them from friends for an hour or two at a time.

I'd been able to lean on Amelia and Eva in high school, but that safety net was fading away and I felt more alone than ever. I'd wanted so badly to prove that I could take care of myself. That I didn't need anyone. That I was a grown-up. By the time I admitted to myself that I *did* still need others, I'd pushed away the people I loved.

Depression is different from sadness; it's not how you feel after getting dissed by a friend or fighting with your siblings. Those things hurt, of course, but even amid the agony, you know there'll come a moment when the heaviness lifts. Depression, on the other hand, can feel like the absence of hope. It's a long, flat road with no horizon in the distance. It's the path my brother once walked.

This is the story of a night I'll never forget.

Forecasters had predicted snow, and on the evening of December 13, 2007, it arrived. By nightfall, the city's bustle had quieted to a murmur and Boston slept under a thick white blanket.

The time on my phone read 2:52 a.m. Every inch of me throbbed. If only I could fall asleep.

I slid from beneath the covers and wedged my feet into my slippers. I put on my coat and tiptoed out to the hallway. As if in a dream, my body led the way to the staircase to the rooftop. Slowly, I climbed. *One flight. Two. Six. Eight.* Icy air stung my face when I reached the terrace. I clutched my arms around my chest for warmth. Snow glittered on the gray cement. I looked out over the neighborhood. Eerily silent and beautiful.

At the building's edge, I sat down, inching forward until my feet dangled over the side. I poked my head over the ledge and stared down. A parking lot, mostly empty, was below. I imagined falling, flying through the air. Then landing heavily on the ground. The finality of it gave me a chill up my spine.

Tears rolled down to my chin. A spool of thoughts ran through my head. *I'm useless. I'll never amount to anything. I'm not smart enough to get through school. How can I help Mami and Papi when I can't even help myself? The world would be better off without me in it.*

I'd been telling myself that life would look up, that tomorrow would be brighter, but all I could see was darkness with no way out. From my perch on the edge, I thought: *Am I really ready to do this?*

My lids grew heavy with exhaustion. With my legs still swaying over the ledge, I lowered my upper body onto the cement and dozed off. I don't know how long I slept like that, but a strong wind gust awakened me suddenly.

Where am I? I pushed up onto my elbows and gazed around, confused about why I was on the rooftop. Then all at once I remembered in shock. *My God, what am I doing?* My stomach sank. I scooted backward and tried to stand, but as I did, the bottom hem of my coat got caught on a nail. *Rip.* I lost my balance and teetered forward over the building's ledge. My lower body dangled just above a window. *Boom. Boom. Boom,* went my heart. Gasping, I clasped the pavement, but slipped another inch. Desperately, I tried to balance my feet along the window's top edge, but it was too thin to hold my weight. So with every cell in my body, with every ounce of strength I could muster, I used my upper body to hoist myself up.

Flop. My body stumbled back to the safety of the rooftop. I dropped down cross-legged in shock. Hours before, I'd been desperate to take my life. In that split second when my body slipped out of my control, my impulse for survival jolted me awake. Tears overcame me. A vision of Mami and Papi flooded my head. They'd endured so much heartache. They'd put it all on the line to come to this country so I'd have a chance to make something of myself. I could not let all they'd given up for me go to waste. I owed them more than this. They'd paid too great a price for me to throw my life away so senselessly. It wasn't time for me to go. Not like this.

My twenty-second birthday in Boston

Birthdays in Colombia

16

TURNABOUT

It's hard to predict how deeply people can affect us. We exchange BFF bracelets with friends, love notes with crushes, laughter and tears with family. If even *one* of those people has a lasting impact on us, we're fortunate. Lorraine was one person whose impact I never saw coming.

I met her shortly before the roof incident. The self-harm is what led me to her doorstep. I did most of it in private, but David noticed. Our relationship was rocky, but he did his best to pull me from my crisis. "You need to see someone," he would say. I'd grimace, thinking, *Yeah right, bro.* Finally, I agreed. One evening when I was particularly despairing, I googled "low-cost clinics in Boston." Near the top of the results was the name of a center in my area. I called and made an appointment.

The next day, I showed up at the clinic and plopped down in the waiting room. Next to me was this young Asian dude who was on his phone; across from us sat a blond woman flipping through magazines. They both looked normal and cool. Maybe I wasn't a freak for coming here, after all.

Seconds later, a Latina woman stepped out of a swinging door. She was around five feet three, probably in her midforties, and rocking cute skinny jeans and a fitted blazer. Ringlets of short black hair framed her round face perfectly. She had on a pair of stylish glasses. *Nice*, I thought. *This might work.*

"I'm Lorraine," she said. Her eyes were bright, her expression warm. She seemed cordial, not that phony kind of friendly. "You must be Diane," she said. I followed her back through the swinging door and down a long hall to a corner office.

"So what brings you in today?"

I cleared my throat and sat up.

"Well," I replied, "things have been tough lately." I glanced down at the rows of fresh cut marks on my brown skin. She looked, too.

"What's been happening, hon?" she asked.

"I've been cutting," I told her. Before I could continue, tears tumbled from my lids. It was the first time I'd heard myself say those words out loud.

Lorraine didn't appear to be offended or surprised by what I told her. In fact, she scooted closer to me.

"Why do you think you cut yourself, Diane?" she asked.

"I don't know," I sniffled. "I guess it feels better than all the other stuff I feel."

"What other stuff is that?"

"Just everything," I said—and right there, in a flood of emotion, the whole ugly mess of the past six years came spilling out: The afternoon I returned to an empty house. Visiting Mami and Papi in jail. How frightened I'd been in the months following my parents' deportation. The stress I was under to take care of myself while keeping up with school. The debt I was paying off. Missing Mami and Papi, and feeling guilty for avoiding them. The big responsibility I felt as their only hope for returning to America.

Lorraine sat back in her chair. "Diane, what you're feeling makes so much sense," she said. "When your mother and father were taken from you, you were forced to become your own parent. That's an enormous load that no fourteen-year-old child should have to carry. It's time for you to put down that burden." She then stood, gently pulled me up to my feet, and hugged me more tightly than I've ever been hugged.

By the end of our meeting, I felt stunned by how much I had revealed. It had been so long since I had opened up that much to anyone.

"You're going to be okay," Lorraine reassured me as I left. "We'll get through this."

I'd love to tell you that our session was enough to

immediately straighten things out for me. Lorraine couldn't wave some magic wand and, poof, make everything go away. But she clearly cared what happened to me—and knowing that someone was right there to talk gave me hope.

In another session, I admitted to Lorraine, through tears, that I'd tried to end my life that cold night in December. I hadn't told anyone what happened, not even David. The night on the roof was not about getting attention—it was a quiet moment between God and me when I had to decide whether I would go on.

Lorraine looked thoughtful, then gave me some tough love: "Diane, we'll need to focus heavily on behavior changes— because I do believe that you can change."

Psh. *Yeah, right*, I thought. But a small part of me, little Diane who had big dreams, hoped that she was right.

In the summer of 2008, I graduated college. The depression I was still struggling through made it difficult for me to even feel proud of this accomplishment. There I was, out in the real world, having received the education my parents always wanted for me. But I was also in debt from the cost of school—and still unsure of what kind of work I could do to not only pay for my own life but also pay for my parents to get a lawyer. So I earned fast cash working at a nightclub. The low point of that job was serving gross customers; the high point was hanging out with the other girls who worked there.

The doors opened at ten, but the party really began popping off at eleven. I threw back drinks to maintain my energy—a not-so-great habit for someone who'd struggled with drinking and partying over the past few years. But drinking was how I kept myself from noticing how sketchy the whole scene was. I tried to seem upbeat. You could call it my first acting gig—and let me tell you, I was so convincing that I should've earned an Oscar. In my heart, I knew this was a terrible environment for me, but on my face was a glowing smile.

During our breaks, I'd crack my coworkers up by singing and dancing, imitating Britney Spears dancing in the video *Stronger*. Oh, and let me tell you, I hammed it up. I would make my voice high, wildly swing my hair from left to right, and do these insane moves all over a chair the way she does. They all laughed hysterically.

"Diane, why aren't you trying to be an actor?" my friend Luciana would ask. "You could totally be on TV."

But I had a different plan. During this time, I enrolled in a paralegal program, thinking that if I became an attorney, I could one day represent my parents' case, and others' in their situation. To make more money, I also took a part-time receptionist position at a law firm. Week after week, I sat there at that desk job, answering phones and filing documents. Real talk? I have never been more bored in my life. The minutes literally dragged by.

The year after college was like a juggling act. Between balancing paralegal work, waitressing, and being a receptionist, I was barely sleeping. I'd been taking care of myself since the age of fourteen, and frankly I was sick of it. With all my heart, I wanted to go back to the days when I felt safe. When the smell of Mami's rice and plantains greeted me at our front door. When the sound of Papi's laughter made me feel like the most precious girl in the world. But I couldn't go back. The only way out was ahead.

Through the nonstop busyness, I still made time to see Lorraine. And I wasn't hurting myself as much. "When you have the urge to cut," Lorraine had advised, "squeeze some ice in your hand instead." Believe it or not, that worked for me.

One session, I vented about my work.

"I used to think I wanted to be a performer," I explained. "I'm now considering law."

"What made you change your mind?" she asked.

"A career in the performing arts isn't practical for me," I told her. "It's too late. If I wanted to be in musical theater, I should've gone to a conservatory."

She removed her glasses and placed them in her lap, then looked right at me. "My dear," she said, "do you think you're just afraid that if you went after that dream now, you'd fail at it? It may be why you set up these roadblocks for yourself."

I squirmed in my chair. "What roadblocks? What do you mean?"

"I mean that you get in your own way, whether or not you're aware of it," she explained.

"I guess so . . . ," I said, taking it in. "But I'm not even sure I still wanna be an entertainer."

"Really?" she said, raising her brows. "You light up every time you mention it."

I shrugged. "I may not be good enough." Entertaining my friends was one thing. Making a living and putting myself out there in front of the world was another matter altogether.

"I think you're allowing fear to block your greatness," Lorraine said. "You've gotta change your mind-set." She had a point. Fear is what had kept me from applying to a conservatory. Law was the safe option, though, right? Or was it a detour from the route I was too frightened to take?

Most of my moves had been based on the fact that I was scared out of my mind. What if I did everything in my power to become a success and bring Mami and Papi back here, only to fail miserably at both? What if I pursued an acting career and got booed off the stage? What if people didn't like me? In many ways, I'd been avoiding my dreams so I wouldn't have to find out.

I'd spent my entire childhood trying to be the Good Catholic Girl. Trying to earn the approval of others, even those who called me horrible names like "wetback." Trying not to make the mistakes my brother made. Trying to get my parents back in the States. Trying to show everyone that

I wasn't going to be *that* kid—the one who fell behind. The fact that I'd at last thrown up my hands to the world made me, in my own eyes, a total screwup. But in Lorraine's view, it made me a human being—one who deserved to be here, whether or not I did another thing right. What a revelation.

In November 2009, almost two years after that night on the roof, I made not one move but three of them. I quit my job at the club. I enrolled in an acting course at Boston Casting. And I started searching for auditions.

Peter Berkrot's beginner acting class at Boston Casting

17

STAGE RIGHT

So how do you find your passion? Your true calling. Your career path. In a way, I believe that you don't choose your life's work; it chooses you. From dawn to dusk, you can think of nothing else. It's like a crush who finds their way into your daydreams and diary entries. You find yourself talking faster, louder, more excitedly upon its mention. When I finally gave in to my desire to be an actress, I felt all of the above.

At first, I didn't want to discuss my goal with anyone. I thought talking about it might jinx it—I'm a bit superstitious that way. Since childhood, I was in the habit of keeping secrets, whether it was protecting my family's status or safeguarding my dreams. I was always scared that my desires were out of my league. That if I opened up about them, I'd be laughed at for even thinking I was capable of greatness.

But here I was, doing my thing. First of all, I enrolled in two courses: beginning acting and improv. My teacher was Peter Berkrot, who was in *Caddyshack*, that classic movie starring Bill Murray. The other students were from all different backgrounds. There was this one lawyer who wanted to use acting techniques in the courtroom. Another guy had been in a few indie flicks. And there were plenty who, like me, were new to the world of acting. I could hardly contain my excitement. I went from sleeping all day to waking up early in anticipation of all that I could learn. Our passions don't just compel us; they can also heal us.

I absolutely loved improv class. Peter would throw out a random scenario, and each of us then had to step into the character and situation and run with it. So fun! It all just poured out of me. Within seconds, I'd come up with drama and dialogue. "You really performed that powerfully, almost like you'd lived it," Peter would tell me afterward.

The positive feedback kept me going. Once class was over, I'd stick around so I could pick up any extra tips Peter might have. "You know, you're good, Diane," he once told me. "You'll have to keep working hard at this, but you do have a gift." He also urged me to be less shy. "Forget about looking silly," he'd say. "You've gotta get over your inhibitions so you can fully embody the character." As I followed his advice, my confidence grew. I began to actually call myself an actor. Not necessarily out loud, but in my head—which is a start.

As much as I loved these classes, they were each only once a week. Which meant that the rest of the time I was working at the law firm and at a new bar. Creditors were still blowing up my phone, and I had bills to pay. Could I one day make enough money just from acting? I wondered. I didn't even need to be rich; I still just wanted to be able to pay for a lawyer for my parents.

So I auditioned. *A lot.* I swear, I tried out for approximately one billion short films and music videos. One of the first parts I got was in a music video with a Boston R & B singer called Louie Bello. The whole time, I was supposed to stare at Louie and give him doe eyes! It was corny, yet I was appreciative, because, hey—it got me on camera. My second video: I played a vampire in this rock 'n' roll video called *2 in the Morning*, directed by Stephen Vitale. *Raaar.* Biting necks suited me better than being just another cute girl. I was ready to show the fire in me.

I didn't even get paid for some of these parts, but I figured they would give me experience and something to show for myself. Like a role in a short horror indie flick produced by my friend Billy Dufresne. The film was awful, and we filmed the whole thing in Billy's backyard—but we were all so passionate that it didn't even matter. My character got locked in a basement. I had to wave my arms and scream the whole time. As ridiculous as it was, I immersed myself in the role and pushed myself to take it to the next level.

Next, I scored a job as an extra in the background of a scene in *Zookeeper*, the romantic comedy starring Kevin James. But standing to the side wasn't my thing. I was like, *Are you kidding, boo? I'm an artiste.* I did not, repeat *not*, want to be a so-called background artist.

And just like that, as my fervor for my work increased, the depression and drinking habit fell away. Two things saved me emotionally. One was seeing Lorraine, who encouraged me to open up about my pain as well as about my passion. And the second was returning to the arts. Finally, I knew what I wanted to do with myself.

I had headshots taken—they're basically pictures from the neck up that showed me smiling. I uploaded my photo and résumé on every acting site that I could. For weeks, nada. But in the fall of 2010, I got my first official audition: for a part in a Kmart commercial.

"Oh my God, I can't believe it!" I shrieked when I heard the news. I'd been given three lines, something cheesy like, "These cotton T-shirts are incredible!" You would've thought I was auditioning to be in the next *Star Wars*.

On the morning of the tryout, my excitement turned into terror. What should I wear? What should I say? Would they like me?

The waiting room overflowed with all sorts of folks, some

brunette and lanky, some short and burly. I was one of only a few Latinas. I couldn't help comparing myself to everyone.

One at a time, the actors were called in. The casting director, a goth chick with a clipboard, at last called my name. I sat up and straightened the cute dress I'd so carefully chosen.

"Come right on in," she said, leading me to a room.

A group of casting directors sat in a semicircle. No one cracked a smile. The goth lady explained the commercial and handed me my prop, a pink tee to be featured in the ad.

Well, here it goes. I cleared my throat and stood up tall. "These cotton T-shirts are incredible!" I said, practically burning my cheeks off from smiling so hard.

The group sat silent. "Okay, great," the woman finally said. "Let's hear your other two lines."

I delivered both flawlessly, and again, they stared blankly. "That'll be all," the main woman told me. "Thank you for coming in."

Yikes. No feedback? No praise? No dis, even? Harsh. Three days later, my big break became my heartbreak. I didn't get the part. I tried not to let it sour my mood, but it stung.

"You never know what they were looking for," my teacher Peter consoled me. "It could've been something as random as they didn't think you were the right height, or they decided to use a guy instead. You just have to keep going!" Sigh. Rejection hurts, but I knew what I was getting into when I started auditioning. Next big break, here I come!

My classmates became my new circle of friends, especially these two cool actors, Dan and Kathy. The three of us were inseparable. Through Dan, I met Rebecca Rojer, a film student at Harvard. She was auditioning a bunch of people for the main part in her short film called *Ashley/Amber*. "I don't think I'm ready for that," I told him. I'd peeped at some of Rebecca's other video and film work online. Her stuff was intimidatingly good. The audition was on Harvard's campus. That fact alone was nerve-racking.

"You should try out," Dan urged.

Having people who pushed me, who cared enough about me to give encouragement, meant the world to me. I agreed to go if Dan promised to come with me. On the day of the tryout, it snowed. As we walked past the ivy-covered buildings and gold steeples, my mind flashed back to all those Sundays when Papi drove us through ritzy neighborhoods. It was a secret, elite world I never thought I'd be part of, and yet there I was.

"This is awful," I told Dan, as we cut across an icy Harvard Yard—more out of fear than anything else. "I wish I'd never signed up for this. I don't even know what I'm doing here."

"Calm down," Dan told me. "You'll do fine."

Rebecca called me in almost right away. "How are you, Diane?" she asked, extending her hand. She seemed supernice. *Phew.* "I'm great," I said. Dan shot me a thumbs-up as we went off into a small studio. It seemed to go . . . okay?

From the Kmart crew to Rebecca, I couldn't tell *what* they thought of me. Rebecca surprised me as I was about to put on my coat.

"I appreciate you coming in today," she said, "and it'd be great if you could come back."

What? Did I hear her correctly? Is this a callback even before I've left the building? "Um, all right," I said shyly-slash-exploding-with-joy.

"How about next Wednesday?" she asked.

"Sure," I answered, cool as a cucumber. OMG.

When I returned the next week, I freaked. To my right sat a knockout brunette and a gorgeous blond with perfect teeth. I wouldn't stand a chance against that Jennifer Lawrence look-alike over there. *I'm so not getting this.*

When Rebecca brought me in a few minutes later to recite lines, I did my thing—and I held nothing back. "Wait here," she told me afterward. She disappeared from the room and returned a few minutes later wearing a big smile. "I'd love to have you do the part," she said. The room stood still. "Really?" I squealed. "You would?"

"I think you would be a perfect fit," she said.

I was stunned. Literally. "I'm so glad Dan connected us," she continued as I stood there gaping. "I'd already auditioned a hundred girls for the part and couldn't find the right person."

I left that room and called Dan. "She wants me!" I

screamed. "Thank you so much for pushing me to do this!" It blew me away that I'd been picked out of so many girls. At *Harvard* no less. At last, I was getting something right.

Working on *Ashley/Amber* is still on my top ten list of most fun experiences. I was the main character! In the film, which is a dark comedy, Ashley and Amber are the same person, which explains the slash. During filming, everyone in the cast had to pitch in. We shot at Rebecca's place, at a café, and sometimes even inside my apartment. We also did a lot of outside shots, in the snow. The whole thing was very crunchy-granola, um, I mean artsy.

Being on camera was such a rush. I was *soooo* serious, probably because I was fresh and nervous. I wanted everything to be perfect! But Rebecca was thrilled with the performance, and the film was screened at the Berlin International Film Festival. I even got to travel to Germany to the premiere.

Then, early in 2011, an amazing opportunity arose. I got an audition for the ABC series *Body of Proof*. I had to act out driving and falling asleep at the wheel; when the character awakens, she realizes she's run over someone and is later arrested. The same day I did the audition, the unimaginable happened: I got the part! I swear I almost did somersaults.

A couple of weeks later, we traveled to Rhode Island to shoot the scene. I had a trailer and a hair and makeup team. Let me tell you, I felt like I'd arrived. You know how on *Law & Order* the first scene sets off the whole episode? That's how it was on *Body of Proof*, and my scene was the show's opener. I rewatched it on loop. All I could think was *That's me! That's really me!* I started getting e-mails from people in Colombia. "I just saw you on TV!" my aunt wrote. Knowing that my family was proudly watching meant everything to me.

I thought back to those nights at the dinner table, performing for my beaming parents. Yes, we were distant now, but I still felt grateful that through everything, they had always supported my dreams. Their faith in me was part of the reason why I was pursuing what I loved.

Many times in our sessions, Lorraine would ask me, "How does it feel to be in front of the camera?"

"I feel free," I told her, "like I can do anything."

Performing is one of the scariest things ever, but the fear is part of the thrill. And when you get it right, this rush just comes over you. I'd had that rush in high school, when I'd performed at spring fest, and then again during my senior recital. Every time I got into character, I felt powerful. To this day, I still haven't gotten over the exhilaration of performing.

In my gut, I knew I was ready for my next life move. David and I decided it was time for us to split. Life was clearly moving me toward the mecca of the acting world—New York City. As they say, if you can make it there, you can make it anywhere. I wanted to prove to myself and the world that I had what it took to do this thing.

Me and the shiny Big Apple

18

NEW YORK CITY

Diane . . . is that Gwo-WHERE-way? How do you pronounce your last name?"

"It's Guerrero," I said, trying to keep up my fake smile. *It's really not that hard to say*, I wanted to add with a grimace, but didn't.

"Well, whatever," she said. She was a talent manager a friend had recommended I visit, a small, old Italian lady with one of the thickest Brooklyn accents I've ever heard. "Here's some dialogue for you to read for me. Have a quick look and then shoot."

Please, brain, do your thing. I took a deep breath, stood up straight, and delivered the lines as smoothly as I could. She stared at me without batting an eyelash. What is it with people in the biz and not smiling?

"The thing is, honey," she said. "I don't know if you're pretty enough for this business. But yeah, I guess we'll give you a try."

'Scuse me? "Uh, all right," I said. "That sounds good." In spite of her rudeness, I gave the rest of my lines and slayed it. As I left her office a few minutes later, I hoped I'd never see her again. *Thanks for the vote of confidence, you witch.*

It was my first month in New York, and I was quickly learning that the process there was way more brutal than it had been in Boston. I went to auditions constantly. I'd turn up and absolutely give it my all. Then I'd wait by the phone for days and hear nothing.

By this time, I'd found a bartending job in midtown Manhattan and moved in full-time with my aunt Milena in New Jersey. It was a tight space, with only enough room for a twin bed, a TV, and a dresser, but I was grateful she wasn't charging me rent. Being there also meant I could hang with my extended family. When I dragged home late in the evenings, my aunt would often be up waiting to offer me dinner. So sweet. But being home with relatives didn't help with the fact that I hadn't seen my closest family—my parents—in years, and couldn't have felt any farther from them.

Despite things not working out perfectly yet, I knew I was meant to be there in New York. The place pulsates with energy, openness, and possibility. In the city that never sleeps, I quickly learned that I'd better not, either. That's why I signed up for classes at one of the most well-respected acting schools in the city: the Susan Batson Studio in Times Square.

My teacher was this whip-smart, fiery woman named Marishka. "How's everyone feeling today?" she asked at the first class. Scanning the row of faces, she nodded toward the first person in our semicircle.

"I missed my train on my way here and almost didn't make it," one Brooklynite named Ethan offered. "So to be honest, I'm feeling out of breath right now." A few of us snickered. Marishka smiled approvingly and shifted her gaze to the next person in line—me.

"Diane, what's your energy right now?" she asked.

I glanced around at my classmates, twirling the bottom lock of my hair. "Um, I guess I'm kinda jittery today," I said, keeping it vague. "My mom left me this insanely long voice mail this morning, and, well—you know how it goes with family." Everyone laughed, and one or two bobbed their heads understandingly.

Marishka made her way around to the others. One girl had just lost her beloved cat and was overcome with grief. An older dude, a retired dentist, was overjoyed after getting a part in a commercial. And a redheaded woman, a mother from Queens, told us she was feeling "pretty blah."

Free emotional expression—that's what our coursework revolved around. Why? Because great acting is also about getting so comfortable with your own feelings that you can

197

understand those of the characters you play. Marishka called it "sense memory" work.

"Think about the time in your childhood when you were most vulnerable," she once told us. "Close your eyes and imagine that you're back in that very moment. Notice how your body feels." Thoughts of Mami and Papi flashed through my mind. The empty apartment in Roslindale. The sight of Erica in the park, all those years later. By the end of it, I was twisting in my seat. I think it was intense for everyone else, too. Some people were in tears.

During this time, by spring 2012, I'd at last saved up for my own place: a cute, cheap little apartment in Hoboken, New Jersey, a quick train ride from the city. It was so small that I hit my butt on the radiator whenever I got out of bed. But hey, it was all mine. I could come and go as I pleased. After all that deep thinking in class, I could sit in peace and reflect.

The main thing on my mind was how I hadn't seen my family in Seven. Whole. Years. "What are your emotional barriers?" Marishka would ask us. "What walls do you still have up?" I thought about what that meant. What was I avoiding? What kinds of things did I push to the back of my head? What kinds of things did I not want anyone to know about me?

Every answer came back to the subject I'd wanted to avoid since I was fourteen—my family's breakup. My parents may as well have been on Neptune; that's how far away they felt. I knew they adored me as much as any parent can cherish a child, and yet I felt like I didn't belong to them anymore. And though I loved New York, I yearned for a familiar place I could go to when things got rocky.

Week after week, class after class, whenever I'd try a scene, I'd feel myself clamping up. The closer I got to being vulnerable, the more I shut down.

In late 2012, I found myself at a crossroads. I knew that in order to move forward in my life—to continue growing as an actor and as a woman—I needed to go and see Mami. We had some stuff to work out, she and I. Deep down, I judged her, and I held her most responsible for the mess our lives had turned out to be. In my mind, my father was the hero of our family's story line—and I'd cast Mami as the villain. I wanted to see Papi, too, of course, but I've always had a more complicated relationship with my mother and it needed mending ASAP.

"Mami, I'm coming to see you," I called to tell her early one Friday morning. The line went silent, probably because she was twice stunned: first, that I was calling, and second, that I was planning a two-week trip to visit her. "That's wonderful, Diane," she said, her voice shaking. "It'll be so great to see you."

In October 2012, I boarded a flight to Madrid, Spain. Most of the way there, I stared dreamily out the window, wondering how my mom would be different. So many years had passed since our last meeting that I felt like I was going to see a stranger.

When we landed, I wheeled my suitcase through the waiting area's sliding doors. "Diane!" I heard. "Over here!"

There she was. "Oh, sweetheart!" she said, squeezing me long and hard. "It's been so long!" I blinked back the tears and peered at her, taking her in. She even *looked* different: fit, tanned, and toned, like she'd been hitting the gym daily. She was rocking a pair of dark-wash jeans and a cute blouse. Her hair was long and shiny. Her complexion glowed. She looked happy.

Fresh tears welled up in my eyes. Right there in the airport, I began to sob. Seeing how much my mother had changed made me painfully aware of just how many years I'd locked her out. How much of each other's lives we'd missed. How weak I'd allowed our mother-daughter bond to become. Our lives had moved on without each other. How could I have let that happen?

Mami, as if reading my mind, hugged me even tighter than before. "It's okay, hon," she said. "I'm here now."

From that first moment, it was clear to me that I wasn't just there to reconnect with the mom who'd raised me; I was there to meet the person she'd grown into since. Her life in Madrid was so different from the one she had had in Colombia. For starters, she owned a car, one of those tiny models that looks like a toy. The last time I'd seen my mother drive, I was a kid. In Colombia, she had gotten around by bike or on foot. So it was the weirdest thing, all these years later, to see her behind the wheel.

"Let's get outta here," she said, revving up the engine, turning on the radio, and speeding from the lot. She seemed so independent. So spirited and sassy as she zipped through the streets. She changed lanes with confidence, glancing back and forth between the road and me. "So how have you been, my love?" she asked.

"Good, I guess," I told her. I still wasn't sure if I wanted to talk about how I *really* was. Admitting to my struggle with depression over the last few years felt too intense for what was already an intense-feeling reunion.

"Should we stop by the grocery store and pick up anything special for you to eat this evening?" she asked. "I've already made your favorite, *frijoles y arrocito*."

My mouth watered. Boy, did I miss her cooking. "That should be plenty, thanks," I said.

As Mami curved from one road to the next, I peered out at the city. Sidewalks overflowing with people. Little cafés with outdoor dining. Gothic churches and basilicas. Beautifully maintained plazas and squares. Stunning.

Mami lived on the outskirts of the city. "It's not much, but it's home," she said, letting me in. Inside, the one-bedroom had a couch, a table and chairs, and a queen bed and dresser in the bedroom—a palace compared with her homes in Colombia. On the wall hung a school photo of me, at age seven. I had this wide grin with three front teeth missing. I felt a combination of warmth and discomfort when I noticed it. That little girl was familiar yet seemed so distant.

Mami still had to work long hours at her housecleaning job while I was in town, but we spent as much time together as we could. She took me to dinner one night. To a museum one day, then a flamenco concert. She wasn't just surviving in Madrid; she seemed to be thriving. She didn't make much, but it was more than she could earn in Colombia. At long last, she'd regained control of her life.

I've described the great parts of the trip so far—but it was also tough. Just as my mother had grown, so had I. And that meant we clashed. When you haven't seen someone in years, you have to literally re–get to know them, figure out what makes him or her angry, scared, ticked off. Sure, there are plenty of core things that stay the same—but so much can change. And as we made those adjustments, silly tensions arose. "Hang your towel over here on this hook after you shower," Mami would direct.

"Can you not tell me what to do?" I'd grumble back. "I'm not a kid anymore."

Often, she wanted to reminisce about the old days. "You remember how you used to play out in the backyard with Dana and Gabriela while I was cooking?" she asked.

"Of course I do, but that was a long time ago, Mami." For me, those recollections were like old faded pictures, ones I'd tried to tuck away. Mami knew little of my new life—and her mention of the past one we'd shared brought up so much pain.

Four nights before the end of my trip, the two of us sat together on her couch. Mami, speaking more freely than she had before, brought up the deportation. The final one. "That whole time was so horrible for me," she said. "The prison was dirty. I couldn't communicate with your father. I couldn't eat or sleep—"

As she spoke, my blood pressure rose. I sat up and cut her off. "You know what, Mami? I don't want to hear another thing about how hard things were for you!"

Mami, caught off guard, stood. "What are you talking about, Diane?"

"You don't even know how hard things were for me! You abandoned me!" I shouted, standing to point my forefinger right in her face. The words, ones I'd never said aloud, came from some unknown place inside of me, with a fire and fury that surprised me. "You destroyed our family! I hate you!"

Mami widened her eyes, and then all at once, she, too, began to cry. She tried to pull me into her arms. I was weeping so hard that I finally gave in to her pull and buried my face into her.

"Diane, I never wanted to leave you!" Mami wailed. "I

did everything I could to stay with you! Everything! I never meant to hurt you!"

She embraced me for the longest time, rubbing my back and swaying me from side to side as if I were again her baby, her little girl. "I'm so sorry! Please forgive me, Diane! Please, please forgive me!"

I'd spent over a decade making my mother wrong. She might've left that detention center in 2001, but for years after, I'd held her a prisoner, the person most responsible for my heartache. By locking her out of my life, I'd also locked away entire parts of myself. That night, I made the choice to free us both.

On my last day in Madrid, a familiar ballad by Cristian Castro called "Por Amarte Así" came on the radio. We sang together through smiles. Suddenly, I stopped.

"What's the matter?" Mami asked me.

"This song takes me back," I told her, remembering. Before she was deported for the last time, Mami would often spruce up my bedroom, just to make things nice for me. I'd come home from school to find yummy-smelling candles flickering, and sometimes even a present waiting. One afternoon, she'd propped up Castro's CD *Mi Vida Sin Tu Amor* on my pillow. I listened to it on loop. Until we heard Castro's song on the radio, I'd nearly forgotten Mami's gift all those years earlier. I'd carefully buried away the memory along with countless others.

"I've missed you so much, Mami," I told her.

"I've missed you, too, darling," she said.

I cried the whole flight home. The sweet old woman seated next to me handed me tissues. These weren't tears of sadness, though; they were tears of release. Healing and forgiving my mother were the keys to moving forward. And I felt proud of her new life. In some ways, she and I were on parallel paths. We were both reinventing ourselves. Starting over. Rewriting our stories.

My mother had been dealt a whole hand of wild cards in life. She'd played them as well as she could, and she'd managed something far braver than I ever might've attempted at her age. With a heart still burdened from loss and grief, Mami mustered the courage, with Eric on her hip, to set out for a foreign land. A nation where she didn't speak the language. A country that provided a haven from the poverty and violence and despair she was desperate to flee. Along the way, she fell down, got up, and then toppled to her knees again. But in the end, she always got up. And she deserved not my scorn but my deepest admiration.

My breakthrough with Mami had freed up a huge space inside me. I decided to commit myself to staying close with her and Papi. With my spirit so much lighter, I was eager to move ahead with my art.

Just after I'd returned to New York, the Susan Batson

Studio hosted an event for managers and agents to come and evaluate our acting. Here was a chance for a big break. Excitedly, I began searching for a monologue to perform. I settled on one about a girl who had a troubled childhood, married young, and later struggled with addiction. When I read the piece for Susan (yes, the real Susan Batson!), she told me, "This is a nice choice for you. It has a lot of dimension to it." She gave me a couple of pointers, and later that week, I gave a powerful performance, if I do say so myself.

Josh Taylor, an agent from VAMNation Entertainment, approached me afterward. "That was amazing. Can we talk?"

"Sure," I said, blushing. He handed me his card.

Within days of our meeting, Josh signed me up as one of his clients. I had an agent! I can't tell you how excited I was, after months of being told I wasn't pretty enough, fair-skinned enough, talented enough, experienced enough.

Josh began sending me out on auditions immediately. You name it, I tried out for it—from comedies like *Glee* to dramas like *Law & Order*. Afterward, I'd wait by the phone for days, hear nothing—and later discover I'd been up against a real celeb. I once got beat out for a part by none other than Nina Dobrev from *The Vampire Diaries*.

If I didn't get a role, I tried to remind myself that at least the audition gave me more practice, more experience that would eventually bring me closer to my goal. But real talk? Rejection hurts! Young aspiring actors have often asked me whether I ever wanted to quit. Um, how about *yes*. Sometimes daily. But in spite of the struggles, I rolled up in this world as an artist. It's who I am. When I wasn't doing it, I returned to the old struggle of depression and feeling abandoned. So as hard as it was to show up to an endless succession of auditions, I stuck with it.

And believe it or not, this worked. After a while, roles slowly trickled in. I was cast in an episode of *Are We There Yet?*—the TV series created by Ice Cube. I then got the main part in an indie film called *Emoticon ;)* and got to travel to Mexico to film it. I also acted in a movie called *My Man Is a Loser* with John Stamos. A little at a time, I was making a name for myself. "It's only a matter of time before people are really going to get on the Diane Guerrero wagon," Josh always told me. "Just hang in there. Bigger roles will come along."

One week after I'd been turned down for a few parts, Josh sent me a text. "There's this part I want you to try out for," he wrote. "It's a prison series, so don't wear any makeup for the audition, and have your hair messy. Keep it as real and natural as possible."

I read the dialogue that night. The character was named Maritza, this spunky Puerto Rican chick whose rough life has landed her behind bars. In the scene, Maritza is running for prison government, and she gets into a scuffle with her best friend, Flaca. At the end of it, she snaps: "Vote for Maritza if you want more pizza!" *How ridiculous*, I thought. *It's a Web series? Do people even watch those?* Web series just weren't a thing yet in 2012.

The day of the audition, I called Papi for a pep talk. "I'm getting really discouraged by everything," I told him. "It's so hard to keep going to these stupid tryouts."

"You can't give up so easily, *chibola*," he told me. "You're doing your best, right? And that's all you can do. Something is going to work out. Trust me."

Later that morning, at ten, I showed up as casually as Josh had instructed me to. I'd memorized my part the night before, but I kept thinking, *I'll never get cast in anything, not even a Web series.* I delivered my lines for the casting director, Jennifer Euston. Unlike so many others, she actually talked to me afterward.

"That was good," she said, "but I want you to do it again for me. And this time, I want you to make the character a lot tougher." *She must think I'm decent if she wants me to do this over*, I thought. I stood up straight, focused, and launched into my first line. That's when something unexpected happened.

The moment I got into character, I was transported. Back to Boston. Back to middle school. Back to all those times when the girls in my hood got in my face and talked trash about me being "an illegal" or "acting white." My childhood was filled with dozens of Maritzas, and if I hadn't wound up on a different path, I'd be one of them. There, in front of the casting crew, all those experiences were funneled down into my character. Then at the end of the piece, just to add some drama, I put my face right up into the camera lens and yelled out an ad lib: "Yo, f*^#@% *hit* me!" The team looked stunned.

Days went by. No callback. Then a week, which turned into three. My father rang to check on me. "So how'd that audition go?" he asked.

"I think I did okay," I told him. "But I haven't heard anything. So you never know. I don't even care anymore."

"If you gave it your all, you've already won," he said.

No, Papi, I thought. *I haven't won if I don't actually get the part.* I didn't say that to my sweet, supportive father, of course.

You don't move your entire life to New York City to earn the "Great Effort" trophy, right? You don't tuck a blue journal of dreams beneath your mattress when you're twelve because you want to end up in second place. You don't overcome depression and self-harm without wanting to rise up. You take big risks so you can score big victories. You want to be the girl who got the part.

Some of the *Orange Is the New Black* crew

Maritza Ramos

19

ORANGE

It's not every day a girl gets to wear a red bird beak. At a makeup school in downtown Manhattan, I was having my first one ever attached. My friend Kyle was studying to be a makeup artist, and for a class project, she needed a model to turn into a phoenix. Enter, me.

The prosthetic beak was huge and clunky. "Can you hold still so I can get this on here right?" Kyle said.

The beak covered my face so that I could hardly speak—or breathe. "Hmmm-hmmm," I managed to get out.

"This is going to be fly," she punned with a smile.

Just as she was gluing down the edges, my phone rang. Trying to keep my face as steady as possible for Kyle, I answered it.

"Hello?" I managed to mutter, sounding like I'd just stuffed a ball of cotton candy in my mouth.

"Hey, Diane, this is Josh." He sounded out of breath. "I have some news for you. Do you remember the audition for a show called *Orange Is the New Black*?"

"*Orange* who?" I asked. Kyle was motioning for me to get off the phone.

"You know, it's that Internet prison show. And you got it! You landed a recurring role for the character Maritza Ramos."

"Oh my God!" I yelled, jumping up and down. The beak's right edge slid off and dangled over my mouth. Kyle groaned and looked as if she was about to pop me upside the head.

"I got the part!" I shrieked. "I got the part! Josh, are you kidding me?"

"I'm not kidding at all." He chuckled. "In fact, they want you to start filming in about four weeks."

My head spun. "So, like, how many episodes would I get?" I asked excitedly. Kyle, who by this time had caught on that my news was *big*, stood by grinning and high-fiving me.

"We don't know that yet," he told me. "Could be two. Could be five. Could be eight. But you're in!"

Is this actually happening? I kept thinking. *Am I going to be on a show for longer than five seconds?* They didn't want me for just one episode. They wanted me, Diane Guerrero, again. And again. *Whoa.*

By the next morning, bliss had turned to worry. What had

I gotten myself into? What was this whole Web series thing about anyway? Josh had mentioned something about Netflix, but at the time, that didn't mean what it does now. Netflix was still mostly a place to order movies; people watched shows on television, not online.

I was going through the stages that a lot of actors go through: First, there's the zombie stage in which you're totally spaced out and can't believe it's all happening. Then there's the superexcited stage. Then there's the freaked-out "What if I can't deliver?" stage. Followed by the superdiva "Um, excuse me, do you know who I am? I'm *literally* an A-lister" stage. In short, I was a hot mess. But at least I was a hot mess with a job!

Josh gave me the scoop on the series. It had been created by a cool female director named Jenji Kohan and based on Piper Kerman's bestselling memoir. It revolved around a fancy white New Yorker whose past comes back to haunt her and lands her in prison alongside a, um, colorful crew of other inmates. Episode Two, which would be my first appearance— would be shot in New York City. This was starting to sound like the big time.

One month and many sleepless nights later, I turned up at the iconic Kaufman Astoria Studios in Queens at 9:00 a.m. sharp. *Sesame Street* as well as films like *Goodfellas* and *Hair* had been filmed in this studio. *So cool.* I spotted the double doors marked *Orange*.

This is what I found inside: a real film set! Part of me was still expecting it to be a dream, but here it all was. A huge waiting area, with throngs of actors, producers, and background artists milling around. I signed in and then stood there, drooling like a groupie. Famous actors were everywhere: Natasha Lyonne (*Slums of Beverly Hills*). Laura Prepon (*That '70s Show*). Taryn Manning (*Hustle & Flow*). Jason Biggs (*American Pie*). Whoa!

Whenever I'm in a new situation, I get nervous. But I'm sure I wasn't the only one thinking, *How will I ever measure up in this crowd?* I took a seat against the wall, feeling like a shy kid in a crowded cafeteria. From the looks of it, a few actors had already formed cliques. I had no idea what to say or do, which is why I'll always be grateful to the actor who broke the ice.

"My name is Uzo Aduba," said this gorgeous black woman who strutted up to me. She smiled and extended her hand, which I shook. "What's your name?" she asked.

"I'm Diane," I said. "Diane Guerrero."

She sat in the seat across from me. "Where you from, Diane?" she asked.

"Boston, originally," I told her.

"Really?" Her face lit up. "I'm from there, too."

I liked Uzo from that first conversation. She seemed so sure of herself but also warm. We traded stories about Boston, and she told me a little about her family; her parents had come to the United States from Nigeria.

"My mom's, like, my biggest fan," she said. "She was always like, 'Zo Zo, you can do it!' And here I am." On

Orange, Uzo had been tapped to play Suzanne "Crazy Eyes" Warren, a role that would eventually earn her two Emmys and two SAG Awards.

Just as I was describing my character to Uzo, the associate director interrupted to pull me aside.

"We're sending you into hair and makeup now," she told me. I looked over my shoulder to smile at Uzo and stepped off.

The hairstylist brushed my hair until it was silky and then pulled it to the side while the makeup artist started working her magic. Maritza and her Latina crew are supposed to have this ghetto-glam look. Mission accomplished: I could've fit right in on the streets of East LA. Very *chola*-y. Tough and chic.

Next stop: wardrobe. A seamstress handed me a fresh set of those khaki-colored two-piece scrubs. Can I tell you a secret? I love my outfit on *Orange* more than any other costume I've ever had to wear. It's simple and comfortable—like a school uniform. Since everyone else is wearing the same garb, it makes me feel like I'm part of something. And never mind that it's not "fashionable"; I just want to be a serious actor doing serious work.

"We're running behind today," the associate director told me. "Make yourself comfortable. It could be a while." She dropped me off in another waiting area.

I noticed three young women sitting in a circle across the room, cracking up and eating lunch together—and clearly already bonded. I recognized them as Danielle Brooks,

Samira Wiley, and Emma Myles. I saw an empty chair in a far corner and shuffled toward it. I told you, serious shy-kid-in-the-cafeteria vibes. A few minutes later, Danielle got my attention.

"Hey, girl," she shouted, walking toward me. "Why are you sitting over there all quiet?" she said with a grin.

"I dunno," I said. "It's my first day. I don't even know if they're going to use me. Do you think they'll cut me? Do you usually have to sit around for a while?"

She laughed. "Wait, wait, wait—slow down, girl. They'll get to you. Just chill. Come hang with us."

I followed her back across the room, where she introduced me to the others. "Diane's nervous she's going to be cut. But she's not going anywhere. Can we please show her some love?" The girls applauded and high-fived me. *Maybe this isn't so bad*, I thought, sitting down with the crew.

One by one over the next three hours, the actors were called in to shoot their scenes: 2:00 p.m. rolled around. Then 6:00 p.m. Then 9:00 p.m. By midnight, the waiting room was nearly empty. Finally, at 2:00 a.m., my number came up. When I walked on set, several senior producers looked me up and down and then got into a huddle and started whispering. *Oh Lord*, I thought. *They're definitely sending me home.*

"You look too pretty," one of them said.

I raised my brows. "*Hunh?*" I said.

"We need Maritza to be way less glamorous," she explained. "We're sending you back to hair and makeup."

Off I went—and I returned with pretty much a bare face. All the actors in my scene were already on set, waiting. Before I could gather my thoughts, the director called out, "Action!"

Three of the actors in my scene, Elizabeth Rodriguez (Aleida), Dascha Polanco (Dayanara), and Selenis Leyva (Gloria), had worked together in Episode One. They had a rhythm; I, however, had my tongue in my throat. I'd been given three lines to memorize, and I flubbed Every. Single. One. "Cut!" the director kept yelling. *How embarrassing.* We tried it again. And again. And again. Finally, at 3:15 am, the director called it a night.

It took until day three for me to relax. Now I feel completely at ease in the role of Maritza. "Who is she, really?" I get asked by fans and interviewers. "What's her story?" Well, she's a spitfire. She's got a silly side. And she's desperately seeking a family, some security. She's someone who's had to use whatever is available to her, like many others in her situation. Sound familiar?

Maritza's most memorable line is the one I auditioned with: "Vote for Maritza if you want pizza!" Not long after that episode aired, I started seeing Internet memes of myself with that caption underneath it. I swear, people still randomly come up to me on the streets and yell out, "Vote for Maritza if you want pizza!" I felt ridiculous when I said it, which is why it's funny and ironic that it turned out to be one of Maritza's best moments.

A lot of my scenes are with Jackie Cruz, who plays Flaca,

Maritza's best friend. We instantly hit it off. She's so spunky, so fun, so approachable. "Hey, do you want to have lunch?" she asked me that first week. "Sure," I said. That was the beginning of a real friendship, in and outside of work. The directors hadn't initially planned for our characters to be so tight. But when they noticed how close Jackie and I had become, they went with it.

Even if we weren't on a hit show together, I'd hang with Jackie. I can be my goofy self around her. We hang out constantly, whether we're getting our nails done or going for dinner.

Being on set reminds me of my time at Boston Arts Academy. Everyone is creative and enthusiastic. Some days are tough, though. Because I'm reminded that prison *was part of my parents' life*. I picture my mother in handcuffs; my father in an orange jumpsuit. For many on set this was a faraway world; for Mami and Papi, it could not have been more real or painful.

I tried to use these feelings in my acting, the way I'd been taught to do at Susan Batson. Some days, that worked beautifully; other days, I'd end up quietly crying in the bathroom. When my character does things like cleaning or mopping the prison floors, I think of my parents. Long before they ended up in prison, they'd spent years toiling over the most grueling jobs, the ones often avoided by others. Physical labor. They must've felt so trapped, with low pay and zero respect from others. Through it all, they maintained their dignity when others looked down on them or, worse, didn't see them at all.

Orange shines a light on a world that many people in our country don't bother to even think about. It's entertaining and it's also so real. Many viewers write to me and say, "My sister is in jail," or they've spent time in a penitentiary themselves. The disturbing truth is that the United States sends more people to prison than any other developed country, with more than two million people behind bars.

The reality of this suddenly hit even closer to home when my brother called me with some news about his daughter—my niece, Erica. She and I had long since fallen out of touch, and I'd always deeply regretted that. So when Eric told me that she'd gotten caught up with a rough crowd in high school and had ended up in jail, my heart broke. Gloria had done all she could to steer Erica back on track. But with Eric in Colombia, and the struggles of being a single mom in a tough neighborhood, her efforts weren't enough to save her beloved daughter.

I experienced many emotions when I heard about Erica. Guilt that I hadn't been there. Anger that she'd been forced to grow up without the nurturing presence of my parents and the guidance of her father. And sadness that she'd stumbled into such hardships. Here I was, portraying an incarcerated woman and experiencing the happiest moment in my career, while my own flesh and blood was actually imprisoned and living through her lowest point. Sadly, sometimes life and art really do imitate each other.

Accomplishing my goals while my own niece was struggling gave them a bittersweet taste. But while filming Season Two of *Orange*, I got a surprise that'd thrill any actor. An audition for a new show called *Jane the Virgin*, a comedy-drama to air on the CW. The role? Jane, the main character. OMG. Not only might I get to be part of a cool story about a Latina, but I'd earn enough money to hire an attorney to work on my parents' legal case.

A trip to LA and two successful auditions later, my phone rang. It was Jennie Urman, the show's creator. "Well," she told me, "we went with another actor." My heart sank down to my shins. "We all just felt she was the best fit for the part. But—" There was a but? My ears perked up. "We'd like to offer you the role of Lina, Jane's best friend. We think you'd be wonderful for that part."

"Really?" I squealed. Never in my wildest fantasies did I think that I, a girl from Roxbury and a first-generation American, would be considering how to balance *two* roles.

I've absolutely loved my time on *Jane*, as well as portraying Lina. She's feisty, loyal, and likes to par-tay. Working with Gina Rodriguez, who plays Jane, is a highlight of the job. A lot of girls come up to me and comment on how Jane and Lina's friendship is #bestfriendgoals, which I love.

Jane the Virgin feels so special in part because it's a tribute to what is beautiful about Latino culture. It shows a family that loves its Venezuelan heritage but is also grounded and connected to American values. It shines a light on Latin American life that is rarely portrayed on television. This is huge! And the fact that the series has done so well shows how much people want to see Latinos represented. Our stories are part of the fabric of this country. What a joyful way to celebrate who I am and where I come from.

Latinos are the biggest moviegoers in the country. They account for 32 percent of frequent moviegoers. Yet only 3.1 percent of film and television characters today are Latino. That is a problem, considering that 17.6 percent of the population in this country is Latino. In the 168 top-grossing films of 2015 there were only three Latino leads, five Latino directors, and four Latino writers. Out of 1,100 films made from 2007 to 2017, only one was directed by a Latina. This needs to change. Latinos need to start putting their money behind what they believe in. We vote with our dollars and we need to be supporting Latino businesses and art.

When I was a little girl it was so hard to imagine different realistic possibilities of what I could be when I grew up. A lot of that had to do with the fact that I didn't see many brown women on TV or in movies, and I couldn't relate to the stories. I am an American of Latin descent and that story was rarely told. I didn't see a lot of Latin women on TV, period.

I remember the first time I felt represented and like I could pursue a career in entertainment. It was when I saw America Ferrera in *Real Women Have Curves* and Emily Rios in *Quinceañera*. They were among the first to inspire me, aside from Selena. Watching these stories helped me realize that I, too, could be a storyteller.

Only you can give yourself the opportunity in this business—or in any business—by saying yes to yourself. Once I decided to give myself the opportunity, I quickly realized that my job was a lot bigger than acting and telling stories. It's about opening doors. It's about giving young girls a chance to finally see themselves represented. So, once I said yes to myself, I realized that I had to be a voice for others. This pursuit is bigger than just doing what I love. It's about being seen and heard. It's bigger than ourselves.

I can't tell you how many young people have told me how much it means to them to see Latinas represented on-screen. I wish I'd seen the same. Diversity and representation confirms that you and your life are worthy of attention, validation, and admiration. I want every young person—no matter their race, gender, religion, or otherwise—to know in their hearts that their experiences deserve to be talked about, celebrated, and respected.

Life was coming together for me. The truth is, only a few years earlier, I wasn't able to let myself experience joy and success. Now, a space had been cleared in my heart. I'd found Lorraine. I'd rekindled my relationship with Mami. Over time, learning to accept myself—my difficult past, my off-the-wall habits, my true desires—allowed me to believe that others might accept me, too. That I didn't need to hide. That I, like every single person on this planet, deserved love, support, and kindness.

Two hit shows? What more could a girl ask for? Oh, how about a Screen Actors Guild Award nomination for Outstanding Performance by an Ensemble in a Comedy Series? Because in 2015, that's what I and the whole *Orange* crew got. Cue the makeover movie montage; it was time to get dolled up in a stunningly bright red Jill Stuart number and shoes that were as comfy as they were fierce.

Red carpets are both exhilarating and overwhelming. Reporters stick microphones in your face. Bright lights and cameras flash in every direction. Celebs strut and pose. That night, I found myself walking behind Emma Stone and Meryl Streep. I said hello to Keira Knightley. I also mustered the courage to walk up to a certain big actor I won't name, and she gave me this look like, *Who are you, and why should I care?* Hmph!

The affair itself is as glamorous as it appears on television. Swoon! I remember sitting in the audience, holding my breath when that magic sentence was uttered: "And the SAG goes to . . ." It's hard to adequately describe that moment when *Orange* was announced as the winner. I had this mini flashback to that moment when, as a senior at Boston Arts, the crowd applauded at the end of my final recital. That incredible energy in the air, that feeling that makes you want to cheer, "Yes!"

Both of my parents have been lapping up every minute of this wild ride. After the SAGs, Mami called me and yelled, "I'm so happy for you!" Papi congratulated me on the win and mentioned every magazine he'd seen me in. Did the show's, um, R-rated content turn their faces red? Maybe a little, but my parents are pretty open-minded. And besides, as I've come to realize, they'll support me through anything.

Okay, now let's talk Donuts. Earlier, I talked about my love of TV, particularly Nick at Night, where they show reruns of classic American sitcoms. I saw shows like *Taxi*, *Happy Days*, *Laverne & Shirley*, *Married with Children*, and *The Jeffersons*. These were the shows that really informed me as a kid and I think they have a lot to do with my slapstick comedy style. I've always wanted to be in a sitcom and experience a live audience just like on those old shows, and I finally got the opportunity to do that with the show I'm on now, *Superior Donuts*. I can't tell you how happy I am to be on a show like this—a modern-day old-school sitcom. And you wouldn't believe it, I'm getting to work with real live TV sitcom legends Judd Hirsch from *Taxi* and Katey Sagal from *Married with Children*. I've also gotten to work with the amazing comics Jermaine Fowler, Rell Battle, David

Koechner, and Maz Jobrani. And every day I'm learning so much from them.

There shouldn't just be one token person of color. There should be many, to reflect our society, and we need more shows to do this. *Superior Donuts* is one of those shows. It's a twenty-minute comedy about a donut shop owner (Judd Hirsch) and his relationship with his young, artistic, funny employee. And, like any great donut shop, it has its regulars who provide colorful and insightful story lines. This show deals with current societal issues. Every episode takes an opportunity to discuss issues—from gender inequality to stereotypes, race, and morality. It's not like any other show on television.

I play Sofia. She's an enterprising, self-made woman who has poured every penny into her food truck business, which she plans to turn into an empire. I love Sofia because she uses her skills to set herself apart and put her stamp on the world. It's important to represent women in this light—as hardworking, thinking, and innovative people. People who don't have a problem with challenging the status quo.

I love to push myself. I've learned that when you keep your dreams hidden away, they never get the light they need to grow. I'm all about that growth, which is what keeps me slaying every day. I literally cannot wait to see what's around the corner.

Me and POTUS

Diane — It was wonderful to see you! Thanks for getting involved.

20

INTO DAYLIGHT

One day, when Jackie Cruz and I were wrapping up on set, a Honduran woman approached us in the studio parking lot.

"Would you mind if my daughter took a photo with you?" she asked, gesturing to a shy fifteen-year-old with a mouth full of braces.

"No prob!" we said.

After we'd posed with the girl, she cupped her face in her hands and started to cry. "What's wrong?" I asked, worried.

"She's just nervous," her mother explained. "You're such an inspiration to her. She wants to be an actor one day."

Us? An inspiration? It was a sudden reminder that, as an actor, I reach a wide audience; whether or not I realize it, I'm influencing people I've never even met. And I want to use that platform thoughtfully and for good causes.

In September 2014, I had the luck of meeting Grisel Ruiz, an attorney for the Immigrant Legal Resource Center (ILRC), a nonprofit group that helps people who are facing deportation. Grisel educates immigrant families (like mine!) on what they can do to fight deportation. I told her I wanted to put my voice and skills to work. "Why don't you write an op-ed piece?" she suggested, referring to a kind of article that expresses a personal opinion or commentary. "Sharing your experience will keep the country focused on the issue."

Here was a chance to chime in. So for the first time in my life—and a little panicked about what I might've just gotten myself into—I wrote about the day my parents were deported. The story ran on November 15, 2014, in the *Los Angeles Times*, five days before President Barack Obama was planning to make a big announcement about immigration. As I write these words, I'm still astonished by what happened.

Within twenty-four hours, the op-ed went viral. NBC. ABC. *Huffington Post*. NPR. Every major press outlet was requesting a comment from me. I agreed to a short interview with *New Day* host Michaela Pereira on CNN. It was the first time I'd spoken publicly about my family's ordeal. Ever. Even people I've known for years, like friends from high school and college, didn't know about it.

"That seems to be every child's worst nightmare, that your

family is taken from you," Michaela said to me with compassion in her voice. I nodded, and then told her I'd gotten to visit them in Colombia. "How is that?" she asked. That's when my guard went down—or you could say it went flying out the window.

"It's tough," I said, the tears toppling out before I could help myself. "We've been separated for so long that sometimes I feel like we don't know each other. There are things about them that are new, that I don't recognize. It hurts."

Things kind of blew up after that interview. *I've revealed too much*, I thought. *This has been a big mistake.* I'd opened the floodgates for people to judge me. To think they knew all about me because they'd seen one article or video clip. To come up to me in the street or to say crude things about my parents—seriously, who talks smack about someone's parents? But let me tell you, the trolls came rolling in. People wrote awful messages about how my parents should've been shipped back to Colombia years before they were. "In fact," someone wrote, "they should've deported you along with them." Some used racist and sexist slurs. It was deeply upsetting.

Through the darkness, though, I started noticing the other messages I'd received—they were *positive*. Grateful. Encouraging. Comforting. As crippling and toxic as haters can be, there will always be greater power in the good.

The most moving notes I received were from young

people. "I'm so afraid this is going to happen to me," a nine-year-old told me. "What if I lose my mommy and daddy? What will I do?" One sixteen-year-old girl stopped me in downtown Los Angeles and said, "My mother and father were deported last year. I've been on my own ever since." And one woman, though she hadn't been personally impacted by deportation, connected to the feelings of grief and abandonment I'd described. "I lost my parents when I was twelve," she told me, holding back tears. "I know what you're going through."

All these people were here, experiencing what I'd suffered through all along. The more I heard and read, the clearer it became that this was about something much bigger than just my family's tragedy. Millions were living under the radar, ashamed, just as I had been. They, too, deserved a voice.

As I made the choice to step out, I got support from so many people I respect. My castmates, the crew, my friends. "We had no idea you'd gone through this. We think you're brave to open up," they said. That really touched me. Being courageous and speaking out is terrifying—but it can bring you comfort and support that makes it all worth it.

Shortly after the op-ed ran, the White House rang. That's right, President Barack Obama, the forty-fourth president of the United States, invited me to attend his speech on immigration reform. Forgive me, Mrs. Obama, because we all know he's your hubby. But I gotta keep it real: Barack is my boo. All joking aside, I was thrilled—I was going to hear my idol speak at Del Sol High School in Las Vegas, Nevada.

The historic speech was powerful and important. The president stated that deportation relief would be extended to millions. This would lay down the groundwork for undocumented people to work here legally.

Tears stung my eyes as I listened. Oh, Mami and Papi! All the years of worry they'd endured, the thousands of dollars they handed over to that lawyer, and the effort they put into trying to do the right thing. The president's new order might've meant the difference between them still being in this country, and their immediate deportation.

After the address, a White House aide approached me and said, "The president would like to greet you." OMG. The anticipation was overwhelming. I felt like I was floating. Good-bye, gravity!

Just as my turn came up, he said, "I know you." I began to weep. "Oh no," he said. "Don't cry. I've heard your story and I know why you're here. And I want you to know that you're important. You matter."

Then, to my surprise, President Obama mentioned *Orange*. "Michelle and I can't wait for the new season," he told me. *For real? The president and the first lady actually watch the show?* "You're feisty in those kitchen scenes," he said with a laugh. "Don't try anything funny in here—I've got security." Hilarious. He asked a couple of questions about the upcoming season, and I was like, "No, Mr. President—I'm not giving you any spoilers."

A moment later, a photographer snapped an official photo of us, which was later signed and sent to me. "Diane—it was wonderful to see you!" it reads. "Thanks for getting involved. Barack Obama." *Eek!* So cool.

The picture of the president and me ended up on the front page of *El Tiempo* in Colombia, a well-respected newspaper. Mami and Papi had watched everything unfold on television. They'd also seen the viral CNN clip. To be honest, I wondered if I was embarrassing my parents by spilling their trauma. For others, the story was news. For us, it was an agonizing reminder of the fear and separation we'd suffered.

When I asked my mom what she thought, she reassured me. "Tell it the way you want to, and don't be afraid. Use what we've been through to help others."

"Always remember that you're in charge of your own story" was Papi's take. "You get to decide what you want to share. Don't let others push you into talking about anything you're uncomfortable with." That wise advice has served me well. My instinct has always been to protect myself and my family. I want to open up about my experiences, but on my terms.

Being in the public eye has its ups and its downs. Having the job of my dreams does, too, believe it or not. Getting high-profile acting work doesn't mean I'm 100 percent set in Hollywood. I've started exciting projects that haven't panned out—not yet, at least. For example, in 2016, CBS bought the rights to my story and I was all set to executive produce and star in a television series based on my life. This project would be my first introduction to being at the helm of a creative team. Producing *and* acting in a story about family and immigration—let alone my own? A dream. I found myself meeting with network executives and creative influencers, and realizing that I *do* belong at the same table with them.

Long story short, after all the effort and initiative, the show didn't wind up getting made, which was personally and professionally disappointing for me. But here's the takeaway: This is the way show business is. And just because I was told *no* once, doesn't mean it's over. I've learned not to be so attached to things. My motto is to give my work my all, no matter what the outcome will be. It takes guts to make the effort and put yourself out there. Now I'm just even more motivated to rework my story for television, film, or for a streaming service in the future. As long as I continue to create, I know I'm going to keep working.

Recently, I've had the privilege of being able to talk to students across the country about my experiences. We talk about being true to yourself, fighting for what you believe in, and the importance of mental health and immigration reform. I've been inspired by seeing so many young faces hungry to be represented and to find content that actually speaks to them.

This whole experience has inspired me to be not just an artist in front of the camera but an artist behind the camera as well. That means producing and creating stories from the ground up that will empower my community and create opportunities. That is my mission.

Colombia is a complicated place full of poverty and violence, as well as love and culture. Mami is back there for now. Proving yet again that she'll do anything to support her children, she left her comfortable life in Madrid to be with Eric, who has struggled with his own ups and downs. I don't know what the future holds—she still wants to return to America and be with me—but she does have the option of going back to Spain. Now, she and I talk at least a couple of times a week. What a change after seven years of near silence! She's so cute: She'll text me my horoscope, or a photo or inspirational quote. Or articles I've been featured in.

During Christmas 2014, I traveled to Colombia to visit everyone—but especially Papi, whom I hadn't seen since that Christmas during college. Just being together felt special, like those childhood trips to the beach or carnival. He was the same open, funny, and warm father I remembered. One afternoon we took a walk, just the two of us.

"Papi," I asked, "if you were able to come back to America, what would you do?"

He stopped for a moment. "I'd do anything," he said.

"Any job would be okay. Maybe I could find another factory job. Doesn't really matter."

"What do you mean, it doesn't matter?"

He didn't flinch. "I just don't want to miss any more of your life. I only want to be near you. We've been away from each other for too long already." I reached over and hugged him. "I love you, *chibola*," he added. "Always will."

My dad wasn't looking for some fancy life. He simply wanted to be close to his only child. And even in his midsixties, an age when many retire, he was willing to take a lowly job just so he could be around me.

More than seventeen years have passed since my parents were taken. I still long for their guidance—after all, no matter how old I am, I'm always going to be their little girl. I get some of that over the phone, but it's not the same as being together. I daydream about us doing little things together like shopping or picking out a recipe for supper. Though when you think about it, those aren't little things at all. They're the experiences that, one at a time, make up this thing we call life.

These days, not only am I getting along beautifully with my parents—they're also getting along with each other. It makes me incredibly happy. And I'm grateful that I can now help them both out with money—to repay them for all they did for me, and to help them from my position of privilege. My goal is to make their lives comfortable, to visit them as much as possible.

In November 2016, a heaviness hung in the air as the results of the election came in. A month later, shocked and dismayed, I went back to Colombia for Christmas. Despite the turn of events in the United States, Christmas in Colombia was as festive as ever. My family got together at my mom's house—and I mean the whole family. Cousins, uncles, and aunts from both my mom's and dad's sides gathered for a huge meal cooked by Mami, plus cake. In between eating, snapping photos, and playing games (we even did the mannequin challenge, LOL), it suddenly dawned on me that it was the first time I'd ever been with *both* sides of my family at the same time. After Mami and Papi's deportation and then divorce, I'd never expected that I'd get to experience the joys of being all together. To this day, I think of that Christmas as one of the happiest times of my whole life. At the end of the night, after the food was polished off, the table was cleared, and the last relatives left, Mami, Eric, and I sat down together for a cup of tea. In the quiet of the empty home, we wondered aloud about the past, present, and future. We savored the simple ease and comfort of being in one another's company, cracking jokes and sharing memories.

Ever since I was a teenager, I had vowed to do everything in my power to bring both of my parents back to the United

States. In light of the Trump presidency, my strategy has changed a little bit. Here's a painful truth: I don't see them coming back anytime soon, especially with Mami's record of having already been deported three times. So, for now, I'm putting a pause on that effort and focusing on what's going on in the United States. I'm working to influence politicians to pass reforms that will protect immigrants. I'm speaking out in order to challenge people who hold prejudiced and xenophobic attitudes. And I'm looking out for the beautiful, resilient Latin community. I know we can continue to thrive during these difficult times. Supporting one another and advocating for our rights and the rights of others has never been more important.

Right now I'm just happy knowing that my parents are okay and that I can see them in Colombia. I haven't given up hope that they may return to America one day—I just don't think, realistically, that it'll happen with someone like Trump in office. But I'm still working with a lawyer and navigating the process of one day bringing them back, once we have fairer, saner politicians running the country.

The first step to achieving that is getting involved in local- and state-level elections. Let's get as many people as possible in Congress represent our values! When I attended the Democratic National Convention in 2016, I was approached by Sayu Bhojwani, the leader of the New American Leaders Project, an organization that gives first- and second-generation Americans the training and resources they need to run for political office. I want to see more diverse faces out there! Mi Familia Vota is another great political group that gets messages out to the Latino community about bills, voter registration, and upcoming congressional elections. Our goal is to make the 2018 midterm elections as difficult for Trump as possible, by electing Democrats who will fight against his corrupt policies—across the entire country.

Another thing dear to my heart that Trump is threatening to sabotage is arts education in schools. I want every young person in this country to have the opportunity to recognize their own creative potential. That's why I've gotten involved with the Creative Coalition, an organization created by artists, which advocates for arts education for young people. Studying art in school literally saved my angsty adolescent life. It's what got me on the path of becoming an actor. In fact, in 2017, to my delight and surprise, the Boston Arts Academy—my beloved high school alma mater—honored me with the Apollo Award of Achievement, which honors alumni who use their platforms for artistic and social good. From the place that made me the person and artist I am today, I can't think of a higher compliment—or a better motivation to keep fighting for the rights of young people from *all* backgrounds to have access to creative outlets.

I'm also advocating for the need for a Latino museum in

the United States, one that shines a light on how far back Latinos have been a part of this country. Our rich history should be shared and honored.

As fulfilled as I am by my creative and volunteer work, I wish I could tell you my story has a perfect ending. No, I don't have my parents in the States, but I do have them in this world and in my heart. Does it still hurt? Yes. A little at a time, I'm learning to cherish whatever moments we have, even if they're a continent away. The truth is, life is always a mixed bag of triumphs and disappointments, joys and heartaches, random luck and deliberate action. But we do get to choose how we'll walk through our days. Whether we'll cower under our covers in the morning, or rise up to meet the challenges. Lord knows I've done both. And now that I'm a little older, I vote for rising up—as much as we can—for ourselves, for our loved ones, for our communities. For anyone who is treated as a target for bullying, trolls, and even hate crimes.

Shame. Fear. Humiliation. These are all-too-common feelings around deportation. For years, I was firmly under the impression that I was the only person I knew going through it. Now, I'm no longer ashamed, and I'm no longer hiding. Instead, I'm using my voice to advocate for others. To help prevent kids of all ages from going through the trauma I went through.

Trump and his associates continue to incite fear in millions of immigrant families. On January 20, 2017, as he was inaugurated as the forty-fifth president of the United States, he delivered an "America First" speech that was a direct attack on people like my family and me, and millions of others who love our country, honor the contributions of immigrants, and embrace our status as global citizens.

On the following day, distressed but not deterred, I joined eight hundred thousand people on the streets of Washington, DC, for the gloriously peaceful Women's March on Washington. *That*, not the inauguration, was the truly historic event of the weekend. After rallying in unity against hate and bigotry and determined to keep fighting for social justice, the Women's March organizers brilliantly insisted we remain active. I could not agree more: We *must* remain active.

If Trump and his peers think we're going down without a fight, well, that's yet another thing to add to the list of things they are wrong about—and trust me, it's a long list. The Women's March on inauguration weekend was only the beginning. Across this nation, people are showing up in droves to combat the oppression immigrants face—from Latin American and Muslim residents to Syrian refugees. We will not allow an immigration ban to go through. We will not allow there to be a wall built. Undocumented people and refugees have the right to be here, and we will fight to bring them the justice and dignity they deserve. The final chapter in this book is about how to show up for them, with plenty of tips on using your *own* strengths and skills to get involved.

Here's the thing about me and my fellow fighters: We stand united in our goal to make America a place of opportunity *for all*. We share a hope that things can get better. It's the very same hope that once led my family—and so many others—to this great nation in the first place.

CALL TO ACTION

Who am I? I am the girl whose parents were stolen.

My story represents all that should be celebrated about America; only here could the daughter of immigrants go on to college, to Hollywood, and to meet the president. I cherish these opportunities wholeheartedly.

American values include equality, freedom, family, and safety. Why, then, do people in power hound our nation's most vulnerable inhabitants? Politicians threaten deportation. Landlords threaten eviction. Employers take advantage of workers, knowing very well that they can't report abuse to authorities without getting arrested for their status.

The Department of Homeland Security, the branch of government that oversees United States immigration and border patrol, states that in 2013 alone, more than seventy thousand parents of US-born children were deported. That's in just *one* year. Seven percent of kids between kindergarten and twelfth grade have at least one undocumented immigrant as a parent, according to Pew Research. That's seven out of every hundred kids—which is *a lot* when you realize that the United States population is more than 320 billion. Maybe you are one of these kids. I was fourteen when it happened to me.

So what happens to those who are taken into government custody after their parents are deported? Either they are adopted or put into foster care, bouncing from new family to family while dealing with the trauma of losing their loved ones. And how about those young people who are completely overlooked by the government? In the best-case scenarios, they have communities and friends to take them in, like I did. In the worst-case scenarios, they are left to fend for themselves, either slipping into homelessness or left defenseless to the pull of gangs, trafficking, or drug dealing as modes of survival.

There is no excuse for our government to abandon its children. I know that, as Americans, we can do better than that. We can extend greater compassion to one another. And we can push our leaders to listen to and protect those among us who don't have the money or resources to adequately protect themselves.

"Never doubt that a group of thoughtful, committed citizens can change the world," anthropologist Margaret Mead once said. "In fact, it is the only thing that ever has." Millions of people across the world showed up for the Women's March, demanding respect for women's rights, human rights, civil rights, LGBTQ rights, and immigrant rights. I'm fighting for the millions who have the right to reside here. I'm fighting for those who are harassed just for existing, whether it's for their status, gender, race, or religion. I'm fighting to keep families intact. No one should be torn away from their loved ones—nor should a child be left trembling alone beneath a bed.

"People who enter America without papers are breaking the laws," some argue. "It's not fair." It also wasn't "fair" for our ancestors to show up and steal land from the Native Americans, but I don't hear too many folks complaining about the benefits we enjoy because they did. Nor was it fair for our forefathers to kidnap Africans, degrading them and forcing them to build and toil in American fields as slaves.

"Immigrants take jobs from Americans," others complain. "We waste money on them." Nope! The exact opposite is true. Undocumented workers add millions and millions of dollars to America's piggy bank. They contribute to our economy by spending money and paying tax dollars that support our government and our communities. And as far as "stealing jobs"? They are literally doing America's dirty work—cleaning our dishes, offices, and homes, feeding us with the fruit and vegetables they pick as farmers—while living well below the poverty line. Without their backbreaking labor, our country's economic health would screech to a halt.

Donald Trump likes to talk about building a wall between the United States and Mexico to prevent immigrants from entering the country. Besides the fact that a wall would completely destroy farmland, deserts, mountains, and Native American reservations along the border, here's the thing: When people are facing starvation and violence, they will do anything to survive—including scaling a wall or crossing an ocean, as we've witnessed among the Syrian refugees escaping to Europe. If the dangers of staying in one's country are worse than the fear of being caught by border patrol, who wouldn't risk everything to climb over?

Another idea that's thrown around a lot: mass deportation of *all* undocumented people. When immigration officers arrest undocumented people and leave children deserted, families are torn apart and our nation's communities fracture. The truth is, these fractures affect you, me, and every other individual in the United States. Mass deportation would cost between $400 billion and $600 billion, according to the American Forum—and with the loss of all those workers, the nation's GDP (gross domestic product) would sink by more than $1.5 trillion. What an obscene waste of taxpayer money and effort to do something so cruel.

Instead of arguing about whether immigrants should be here—they already are!—let's focus on creating plans that actually move us forward, that allow people to live with dignity. Let's find solutions that are realistic and humane—like putting reforms in place that will keep people safe, our economy thriving, and our culture rich with the creative contributions of diverse voices.

After my parents were arrested, I had no idea what my rights as a citizen were. I didn't know any hotline to call or website to check out for more information on what to do next. Although resources existed, I wasn't aware of them—and even if I had been, reaching out would've meant overcoming enormous fear. I'd been taught to trust no one. There are ways to prepare and fight back, though.

Facing deportation is scary. It feels out of one's control. Sitting down as a family to create a backup plan is a way of regaining some control. "What If I'm Picked Up By ICE in Arizona" is one example of the many excellent state-by-state guides for making an emergency plan (it's written by a team of lawyers in Spanish and English and is available online for free). It urges families to find a caretaker who can take in children, if the worst-case scenario happens. It also suggests parents set up *power of attorney*, which—if they were deported—would give the caretaker permission to make decisions on the child's behalf in place of their parents. This would allow children to stay in their communities and avoid being thrown into foster families with strangers. More tips? Keep a contact sheet with important phone numbers in case of emergency, and collect all relevant legal papers together, in case you need to move quickly. Research lawyers and authorities thoroughly before giving *any* personal information or money away. Check out the resources at the end of this chapter—they may be able to provide more guidance that will make a difference.

The American Civil Liberties Union (ACLU) provides helpful guidelines on their website about what to do if an ICE agent appears at your home. You do not have to let them in if they don't have a warrant from a judge. You can ask for an interpreter or translator, if needed. And perhaps most important, do not sign *anything* without a lawyer to guide you—this way you will avoid agreeing to anything that will harm your chances of staying in the country.

If you're as horrified as I am by the forty-fifth president's administration, you can be more than just afraid. You can get involved. You are *not* powerless, and your input matters. We need your voice, and there are many ways you can contribute. Here are some ideas for simple, yet powerful, actions.

Vote: Once you turn eighteen, vote! Urge friends and family to do the same.

Call your representatives: We can urge Congress to do what's right and oppose bills that are prejudiced and xenophobic. Look up your local representatives and call or write to them. Even if you're shy about talking on the phone, it's actually quick and painless. Try writing a script beforehand if you're not sure what to say (there are also scripts available online).

Donate: Encourage your family, your church/mosque/

synagogue/temple, or your school to donate money to immigrant causes or groups that need funding. Money isn't the only thing to donate, though! You can donate your time, too, and show up for those in need of support, information, or even a listening ear.

Stand up for what you believe in: If you hear someone threatening or insulting anyone because of their status, their race, their gender, their religion—there are ways to intervene safely and calmly. Here's one way: Point out that what the bully is saying is disrespectful or prejudiced. It can often be more helpful to point out what's not right about what they're *saying* than it is to insult them and call them a jerk (even if, let's be real, they're being one). If you don't think it's safe to call the bully out, then reach out to the person being bullied and make sure they're okay, and that they know they have your support. If *you* are the one being harassed—first of all, I am so sorry; you deserve so much better than that. If you don't feel safe telling the bully that what they're saying is offensive, tell a friend, family member, or trusted teacher. Don't carry this weight by yourself!

Listen: Give people a chance to speak—especially the ones whose voices are often ignored. Learn about immigrant experiences from immigrants themselves, not just from the news or the Internet.

Think about how you want to get involved. What are your skills? If you like writing, write an essay to publish in your school newspaper or submit to a national contest to raise awareness about immigration reform. If you like to draw or do graphic design, make signs for activist meetings or events that will benefit causes you care about. If you like cooking, put together a bake sale for your school to benefit people and immigrants in need. If you like computer programming, design a website that draws attention to local immigrant groups or causes. If you like sharing your knowledge, consider tutoring people who have English as a second language and help them master reading and writing. There are so, so many ways to get involved. Everyone brings something special to the table. Feel free to get creative about how you and your friends can put the amazing talents you already have to good use.

And most important, take care of each other. Take care of yourself. Of course, be extremely careful about revealing your or someone else's status in public. But carrying the burden all alone is not an option, either. It hurt my heart to keep everything bottled up and led me down a path of depression and self-harm that I feel lucky to have overcome. If possible, find a friend, family member, or school counselor whom you trust to keep your concerns confidential. You have the right to receive support and kindness throughout these stressful experiences.

I'm not going to deny that this feels like a scary time. But I have hope in the young people around me whose passions are flared up by the injustice that surrounds them. I have hope in the kids who believe in a better future. Let's unite in our desire to leave our planet better than we found it. Every day, I think: How I can turn the trauma of my experience into meaningful change for others? I've chosen to view my ordeal as an opportunity to be a voice for millions. For the sake of all those who come to our shores, I hope you'll join me in that cause.

Want to learn more about the immigration reform debate and get involved? Here are a few resources to support your family, your friends, and yourself:

- Call your elected officials! Find out who they are at: usa.gov/elected-officials

- Learn about running for office someday: The New American Leaders Program (newamericanleaders.org)

- Report and fight hate crimes: Southern Poverty Law Center (splcenter.org)

- Know your rights!

  » The Immigrant Legal Resource Center (ilrc.org)

  » American Civil Liberties Union (aclu.org)

  » Families for Freedom (familiesforfreedom.org)

  » Support the rights of LGBTQ immigrants: Immigration Equality (immigrationequality.org)

  » Support the rights of immigrant children: The Young Center (theyoungcenter.org)

  » Support the rights of refugees: US Committee for Refugees and Immigrants (refugees.org)

- » *Immigrant and Refugee Children: A Guide for Educators and School Support Staff* (from Teaching Tolerance, a Project of the Southern Poverty Law Center) (tolerance.org/magazine/spring-2017/immigrant-and-refugee-children-a-guide-educators-and-school-support-staff)

- » Kids in Need of Defense: providing unaccompanied immigrant children with legal defense (supportkind.org)

- Make a plan.

  - » "What if I'm picked up by ICE in Arizona?" (and other state-by-state guides) (firrp.org/resources/prose/parentalrights)

- Help undocumented people get residency and citizenship.

  - » Mi Familia Vota (mifamiliavota.org)

  - » UnidosUS—formerly known as NCLR (unidosus.org)

- Support undocumented people who have been detained.

  - » Community Initiatives for Visiting Immigrants in Confinement (CIVIC)—End Isolation (endisolation.org)

  - » Detention Watch Network (detentionwatchnetwork.org)

ACKNOWLEDGMENTS

Thank you to my family and friends, who have never stopped believing in me. Thank you to the entire team at Henry Holt and Company, to Macmillan, and to Erica Moroz.

Thank you to all the students who have listened to me speak and to those who have shared their experiences with me. This is for you.